LITTLE LITURGICAL CATECHISM

"This modestly titled work contains most valuable instruction, for children, for the faithful at large, and even for the clergy. It sets forth the meaning of the sacred ceremonies, and is most apt to foster piety by unfolding the significance of all the several parts of the Liturgy."

—**BERTRAND**, Canon of Versailles Cathedral (1859)

"Excellent and genuinely useful."

—**JOSEPH-ARMAND GIGNOUX**, Bishop of Beauvais, Noyon, and Senlis (1867)

"The fruit of serious research, composed with as much method as precision. Through the attentive reading of this volume, the faithful shall no longer remain strangers to the understanding of our religious feasts, our ceremonies, and the manifold details of our sacred worship; and as they shall come to know the origin, the sanctity, and the dignity of these observances, they shall learn to value and to love, for their own sake, those practices which they may have formerly respected without fully comprehending. We commend this valuable work alike to those who instruct and to those who seek to be instructed."

—**AUGUSTIN HACQUARD**, Bishop of Verdun (1867)

"This booklet is very appealing due to its catechetical form. If it were more widely distributed, Catholics would follow the services with greater enthusiasm, and their piety, less ignorant of the liturgy, would be deeper and more lively."

—**FRÉDÉRIC VICTOR DUVAL** (1913)

Little Liturgical CATECHISM

ABBÉ HENRI DUTILLIET
of the Diocese of Versailles

✠

Fifth Edition
Revised, Corrected, and Enlarged with a
CATECHISM OF ECCLESIASTICAL CHANT
by A. VIGOUREL,
Director of Chant and Master of Ceremonies
at the Seminary of Saint-Sulpice

Foreword by
J.-K. HUYSMANS

Translated and Annotated by
STEVEN M. SOLDI, Jr.

OS JUSTI PRESS

Os Justi Press
P.O. Box 21814
Lincoln, NE 68542
www.osjustipress.com

Send inquiries to
info@osjustipress.com

ISBN 978-1-965303-81-8 (paperback)
ISBN 978-1-965303-82-5 (hardcover)
ISBN 978-1-965303-83-2 (ebook)

Book design by Michael Schrauzer

TO MARY IMMACULATE

O Mary,
Virgin conceived without sin,
Mother of our God and Lord Jesus Christ,
deign to accept the homage offered you
in the first of his humble labors
by one of your most devoted children

—H. Dutilliet
8 December 1859,
Feast of the Immaculate Conception
of the Most Holy Virgin Mary

I will go unto thy altar, O Lord:
that I may hear thy praises sung
and tell of all thy wondrous works.

Psalm XXV, 6-7[1]

---

[1] All the psalms found within the *Little Liturgical Catechism* are numbered according to the Vulgate.

Contents

FOREWORD

THAT THOSE WHO DO NOT PRAC-tice the Catholic religion should remain ignorant of her language, her vesture, her gestures, of the entire symbolic economy of the Church, this is easily understood. But what is far more astonishing is that so many of the faithful, though assiduous in their attendance at the Offices, should know neither the detailed meaning of the ceremonies they witness, nor the signification of the words and chants they hear, nor even the purpose of the various vestments and colors employed by the priest in accordance with the liturgical calendar.

How many devout souls, if asked, for example, why the *Gloria in excelsis Deo* was omitted from the Mass they have just attended, or why the priest wears green vestments at certain seasons, would only widen their eyes in bewilderment and confess their ignorance! How few are able to interpret this or that posture of the celebrant as he offers the reconciling mystery! How few are fit to follow, with recollection and inward meditation, the prayerful procession that precedes the Consecration, or to rise with it, after the prostrate silence of the faithful, to accompany the Savior in thanksgiving and glorification unto the consummation of the Sacrifice!

Alas, I fear they are but few. In truth, it must be admitted: among the faithful of our dioceses, ignorance of the Sacred Liturgy is almost universal. And yet, this matter cannot be accounted a light one for Catholics.

As Dom Guéranger[1] so aptly defined it: "The Liturgy is the sum of symbols, chants, and actions by which the Church expresses and manifests her religion toward God." Let us add that the former Abbot of Solesmes further describes it as "prayer considered in its social state."

Indeed, beyond private prayer, that personal supplication we utter in our homes, or at moments apart, within chapels, there exists the common prayer, the universal prayer: that which the Church has appointed to particular hours and composed in definite words. This prayer must not be confounded with the other, and the Catholic is bound to unite himself to it, to make it his own, to pray it.

But can one truly be said to fulfill this solemn duty who, while present in church, fails to comprehend the prayers which the priest utters aloud on his behalf and in his name? I think not. And thus

---

[1] On July 11, 1833, the feast day that marks the translation of the relics of St. Benedict into France, Dom Prosper Guéranger, O.S.B. and his monks (1805–1875) assembled for prayer in a priory church at Solesmes in western France. From there, these French Benedictines received papal approval on July 9, 1837, elevating Solesmes Priory to the rank of an abbey. With Dom Guéranger as abbot, they proclaimed that the Catholic Church, and specifically her liturgy, could help reclaim religion in an age of secularism and revolution. They also encouraged the faithful to follow and understand the words and symbols of the Mass, to sing Gregorian chant, and to participate in the ritual of the Roman Rite. In the opening volume of *Liturgical Institutions* (1840), Dom Guéranger announces his "intention is to produce a movement." In the introduction to *The Liturgical Year* (1841), he emphasizes that the Eucharist is the basis for all true worship as the common offering in which the faithful must unite with what is said and done by the priest at the altar. In 1851, he first used the phrase "liturgical movement" to define the recovery of the Mass in the life and teaching of the Church. Dom Guéranger is widely hailed as the initiator of this movement, which reawakened an interest in the liturgy both among the faithful and French intellectuals.

it may be affirmed that every faithful soul who confines himself to purely personal devotions, and who, for want of having acquired the necessary rudiments, contents himself with repeating the Latin or French of the Offices without grasping a single phrase, discharges only a portion of his obligation and shirks the rest.

Moreover, without this prior study, the long exercises of worship are necessarily devoid of meaning for those who attend them. Hence it is that, during the services, so many appear distracted or weary, while others retreat into private devotions which the time and place do not warrant. Nor could it be otherwise. How, indeed, ought one to be inwardly moved, how ought one's soul to be seized by a spectacle that has become purely ocular, by supplications reduced to mere lip-service? In truth, one is not at home in the holy place if one finds oneself there as a stranger in a land whose language one does not understand.

Truly, those who, for want of the slightest effort, remain ignorant of the science of prayer and rite can scarce imagine the enduring enchantment, the deep and lasting emotion they would experience were they but to follow, day by day, the admirable year of the Church. For they must be told: there is no monotony in the workings of our Mother. All in her worship is full of meaning; nothing is left to hazard; no detail, however minute, is without purpose. Ah, the Church! She has known how to condense whole symbolic systems into a single sign, and also how to unfold in vast cadences, in the most eloquent proses, the least gesture of the Son preserved to us by the Gospels. She is unchanging, and yet ever varied! Behold her Proper of Time, the marvelous diversity of her sequences and hymns, and consider what she offers us, if only we understand: the ability to live, minute by minute, the very life of Christ, to walk beside Him, and, however unworthy we be, to become the diligent companions of God!

And is not the admirable Liturgy the very soul of consecrated buildings, which without her would be but lifeless bodies of stone? Is she not, further, the melodic incense and vocal perfume of the Church herself? Is she not, finally, the echo of Our Lord's own voice?

Behold, then, what power she can impart to our prayers, lending us, in most of her Offices, the very words inspired by God Himself. She knows how to draw forth from the Psalter all the accents of our sorrows and our joys, of our adorations and our fears; she knows how to enfold, as it were, our personal petitions within the great cries and desires uttered on behalf of all mankind by King David. She causes us to speak to the Almighty in His own tongue, expressing our thoughts with grandeur, refining them by her means of utterance, lifting and enlarging our lamentations with her speech. She touches Jesus Himself, reminding Him of those very phrases employed by him who, in the Old Testament, prefigured His coming. And to our prayers thus offered, there is joined, necessarily, virtually, a love, a reverence infinite, such as our private supplications, shaped only by our poor human language, can scarce attain. "But then," you may ask, "if liturgical prayer be thus potent, thus efficacious with God, why do so many Christians deprive themselves of its proper benefit, when they need only open a book that would enlighten them before they go to Mass or to Vespers?"

With one glance, they might be instructed concerning the symbols, the meaning, the end of the offices they are about to attend.

Here, we must needs confess it frankly: the faithful are well-nigh excusable for their ignorance; for the volumes that treat of the Liturgy are, for the most part, ponderous tomes, bristling with marginalia, swollen with references and notes, difficult to grasp for those of modest education, and, what is more, they are of great cost.

On the other hand, the few abridgments devoted to this sacred science are so impoverished in substance that they scarce deserve to be read.

What is needed is a little book, of convenient size, sold at a very modest price, written in a clear and almost artless style, and containing, with plain and detailed explanations, the ceremonies of the Church, unveiling each of their allegories and emblems, defining technical terms, indicating the causes and meanings of the antiphons and proses assigned to certain days, and even setting forth the significance of the objects employed in divine worship. In a word, there is need of a book both brief and substantial, wherein the reader might find, in the space of a minute, the answer to whatever question he may seek to resolve.

Now, such a book does exist: it is this very one.

I discovered it one idle day along the quays. I was weary of groping with my fingers through the dust of bookstalls for paper-wreckage; all I had fished up was a lamentable haul of trifles. I was on the verge of departing when a small pamphlet, buried beneath a heap of mismatched volumes, caught my eye. It was printed in unimpressive type on unassuming paper and bore the title: *Petit Catéchisme Liturgique* by Abbé Henri Dutilliet.

I purchased it, with little hope of having stumbled upon a treasure, but consoled by that modest satisfaction every book-hunter knows when he does not return home empty-handed.

Once seated at home, I opened this little book, and as I read, I marveled at the science compressed into its diminutive pages. I saw, unfolded in methodical order, the most complete and accessible explanations, understandable even to a child, of every pious observance. In that slender volume was compacted, in the form of an essential paste, of a pulp, the substance of massive folios. And truly, I admired the labor of the excellent priest who had dared to undertake, and succeeded in bringing to completion, so rare a task.

I showed the catechism to ecclesiastics well-versed in such matters, and they too held it in esteem. Others, to whom I spoke of it, sought to acquire a copy; but it had long since gone out of print and was nowhere to be found. The author had passed away; the publisher no longer possessed a single copy; no one knew whom to approach to unearth any remnants of the edition, perhaps forgotten in provincial stockrooms or lost amid the bargain stalls of distant towns. In the end, despairing of any alternative, and convinced that this little volume was destined to be of service both to the faithful and to those merely curious about liturgy and sacred art, we resolved to bring it once more to light.

The new edition we here present has been revised by the learned professor of liturgy and plainchant at the Seminary of Saint-Sulpice. To it he has added a short catechism on plainchant, which was lacking in previous editions and whose necessity is now more pressing, since the Benedictines have restored to honor that true music of the Church, so long disfigured, at times, by erroneous notations and, more lamentably still, often replaced in many churches throughout France with theatrical scores and secular songs.

This little book is thus as complete as it can be. As it now appears, it seems to me, at any rate, amply sufficient for those who, without either the desire or the leisure to undertake special studies in liturgy, nevertheless wish to be sufficiently informed to follow with understanding the offices which the Church bids them attend.

J.-K. HUYSMANS[2]

---

[2] Joris-Karl Huysmans (1848–1907), French art critic and novelist of Flemish descent, converted to the Catholic Faith in 1892 because of the Liturgical Movement. His Catholic trilogy, *En Route* (1895), *The Cathedral* (1898), and *The Oblate* (1903), testifies to the extraordinary spiritual power and beauty of the liturgy and sacred art in religious conversion. Within a few months of publishing the first novel, Huysmans wrote a preface for the *Little Liturgical Catechism*, which the Sulpicians revised and republished in 1896.

EPISCOPAL APPROBATIONS

✠

APPROVAL OF HIS LORDSHIP
THE BISHOP OF VERSAILLES

I have read, by order of His Lordship the Bishop of Versailles, the manuscript entitled *Little Liturgical Catechism, or Brief Explanation of the Principal Ceremonies of the Roman Church, for the Use of the Faithful*, and I have found nothing therein contrary to the doctrine of the Church or to the rubrics of the Sacred Liturgy. Nay more, this modestly titled work contains most valuable instruction, for children, for the faithful at large, and even for the clergy. It sets forth the meaning of the sacred ceremonies, and is most apt to foster piety by unfolding the significance of all the several parts of the Liturgy.

Versailles, 16 October 1859
BERTRAND
Canon of the Cathedral

Imprimatur
Versailles, 16 October 1859
✠ PIERRE
Bishop of Versailles

APPROBATION BY HIS LORDSHIP
THE BISHOP OF BEAUVAIS

Bishop's Residence,
Beauvais, 30 November 1867

Reverend Sir,

A most favorable report has been submitted to me concerning your *Liturgical Catechism.* I was already acquainted with the first edition of this work, which had struck me as excellent and genuinely useful. I encouraged you at that time to perfect it further, an endeavor which you have now accomplished with marked success.

I therefore bless this new edition with all my heart. I earnestly hope that it may be widely disseminated among the faithful, who are often all too ignorant in matters pertaining to the liturgy. I shall gladly commend it to the clergy of my diocese.

Accept, Reverend Sir, along with my congratulations, the assurance of my devoted sentiments in Our Lord.

✠ JOSEPH-ARMAND
Bishop of Beauvais,
Noyon, and Senlis

APPROBATION OF HIS LORDSHIP THE BISHOP OF VERDUN

The *Little Liturgical Catechism for the Use of the Faithful* is the fruit of serious research, composed with as much method as precision. Its materials, drawn from the most esteemed liturgical sources, render it a work as profitable to ecclesiastics as to the laity themselves. Through the attentive reading of this volume, the faithful shall no longer remain strangers to the understanding of our religious feasts, our ceremonies, and the manifold details of our sacred worship; and as they shall come to know the origin, the sanctity, and the dignity of these observances, they shall learn to value and to love, for their own sake, those practices which they may have formerly respected without fully comprehending. We commend this valuable work alike to those who instruct and to those who seek to be instructed.

✠ AUGUSTIN
Bishop of Verdun
Verdun, 19 December 1867

TO THE READER

THE KNOWLEDGE OF RELIGION, dear reader, is, as you well know, a matter of great importance; and you also understand that such knowledge brings much consolation. The more one studies this wholly divine religion, the more one loves it, and the more one desires to be instructed in the touching truths which it imparts.

The Church instructs us not only by the solemn and weighty doctrines of the catechism and preaching; she does so also by her chants, her ceremonies, and her festivals. To draw from these means employed by the Church all the fruit she expects, we must learn the meaning she attaches to them; we must learn the language she speaks to us daily to lead us unto God.

This little book is made to aid the devout faithful in their earnest desire to learn. It contains no lofty phrases: it is simple, and it explains in few words the meaning of the feasts, the ceremonies, and the chants of the Church, our Mother.

This brief treatise comprises three parts:

The first treats of the objects used in the worship rendered to God by the Holy Church.

The second treats of the Holy Sacrifice of the Mass, the Divine Office, and some particular applications of the Liturgy.

The third treats of the feasts of the Church, found both in the Proper of Time and in the Proper of Saints.

Finally, we add, in the form of an appendix,

some observations on the most remarkable ceremonies of pontifical functions.

May this little book, dear reader, incline you
to love the holy solemnities of the Church, by
unveiling to you a portion of their mysterious
meanings! May it turn to the glory of God and
the salvation of your soul! If it does you any good,
pray for the one who wrote it.

H. DUTILLIET

Little Liturgical
CATECHISM

❖❖*❖*❖*❖*❖*❖*❖*❖*❖*❖*❖*❖*❖*❖*

Preliminary Notions

1. *What is liturgy?*

The term LITURGY denotes the entirety of the usages and ceremonies of the Church, as well as the prayers employed in the performance of the various ecclesiastical functions.

2. *Is it useful for the simple faithful to have some knowledge of the liturgy?*

Undoubtedly yes, for all these rites were established by the Church to lead the faithful to piety, and they become of no use to those who do not understand their meaning.

3. *Are there several liturgies within the Church?*

Indeed, several have been approved; for example, those of the Eastern Churches. In France, at the beginning of this century,[1] nearly every diocese had its own particular liturgy. Gradually, all have returned to the Roman liturgy, while preserving some local customs.

4. *What then is the Roman liturgy?*

It may be said to comprise the entirety of prayers and ceremonies practiced by the Roman Church, prescribed in the public worship rendered to God.

5. *What is the Roman rite?*

It is the order of office particular to the Roman Church.

---

[1] The nineteenth.

6. *What advantage is there in following the Roman rite?*

By adhering to the Roman rite, one is more truly united in prayer with the Mother Church, sovereign over all others; one performs a more perfect act of obedience to the Holy See, and surely partakes of all the spiritual graces which the Church attaches to the manifold prayers and ceremonies of her public worship.[2]

7. *What is the language of the Roman Church?*
It is the Latin tongue.

8. *Why does the Church pray in Latin in her public offices?*
That all who share the same faith may pray and express their belief in one and the same language.

9. *By what means can the faithful, who do not understand Latin, be edified in the Church's offices?*
By following the prayers in books wherein Latin and French are set side by side, which they may read from time to time, while joining their voices to the choir's chant.

---

[2] The replacement of the local diocesan liturgies in France—all of eighteenth-century composition, and therefore known as neo-Gallican—with the Roman rite was a protracted and controversial process spearheaded by Dom Guéranger. This question recalls the heated debates that accompanied the suppression of these rites.

OF THE OBJECTS USED IN DIVINE WORSHIP

Chapter I

✠

Liturgical Buildings and Furnishings

§ I.
OF LITURGICAL BOOKS

10. *What are liturgical books?*

The books that contain the rules of the cere-monies and the prescribed prayers of the Church.

11. *What are the principal liturgical books?*

There are six: the BREVIARY, the MISSAL, the RITUAL, the PONTIFICAL, the CEREMONIAL OF BISHOPS, and the MARTYROLOGY.

12. *What is the Breviary?*

The Breviary is the book that contains the Divine Office, as it ought to be recited by priests, monks, and nuns.

13. *What is the Missal?*

It is the book that contains the prayers of the Holy Sacrifice of the Mass, intended for the use of the priests who celebrate it.

14. *What is the Ritual?*

It is the book that contains the prayers and ceremonies employed in the administration of the sacraments or in certain other ecclesiastical functions, such as processions and blessings.

15. *What is the Pontifical?*

It is the book that sets forth the order of all ecclesiastical functions proper solely to bishops.

16. *What is the Ceremonial of Bishops?*

It is the book that contains the order of ceremonies in cathedrals and collegiate churches, that is, in churches where a bishop or canons[1] reside.

17. *What is the Martyrology?*

It is a book in which are recorded, according to the day of their feast, the names of martyrs and other saints, as well as the announcement of the principal feasts of the year.

18. *Which liturgical books do the faithful hold in their hands during the Church's offices?*

They are extracts from the Breviary, the Missal, and the Ritual, known as the *eucologe* or *paroissien*, complete *paroissien*, or little *paroissien*, depending on how abridged they are.[2]

19. *In what manner ought the faithful to use these books?*

They must treat them with great reverence, and Christian parents ought to instill this respect in their children by showing them that these books contain the prayers of the Church, and by teaching them from an early age to follow the office.

---

[1] "An ecclesiastical person (Latin *canonicus*), a member of a chapter or body of clerics living according to rule and presided over by one of their number" (*The Catholic Encylopedia* [1908]).

[2] In English, these prayerbooks are known simply as "hand missals" or "missalettes," even though they often include texts from the Breviary and Ritual as well.

§ II.
OF PLACES CONSECRATED
TO WORSHIP

20. *What name is given to the buildings where the functions of the Catholic worship are ordinarily celebrated?*

They are called Churches.

21. *What does the word Church mean?*

In itself, this word means ASSEMBLY, but when applied to Christian temples, it means the place of the assembly of the faithful.

22. *What are the places adjoining the Church?*

They are: the SACRISTY, the CEMETERY, and sometimes the EPISCOPAL RESIDENCE, the CLOISTER, and the PRESBYTERY.

23. *What is the sacristy?*

It is a room adjoining the Church, used to keep the sacred vessels, the ministers' vestments, the Church linens, and, generally, all objects consecrated to the worship.

24. *What ought to be observed in the sacristy?*

Silence ought to be kept there, or at least voices lowered, because the sacristy is part of the church, and it may happen that Our Lord bodily dwells there in some particle of the Host remaining in the sacred linens.

25. *What is the cemetery?*

The cemetery is a small field which formerly surrounded the churches, as can still be seen in many rural areas. Ancient authors sometimes call it the *dormitorium* (the "dormitory") because it is there that we shall all repose in the peace of God awaiting the resurrection of the bodies.

26. *How ought one to behave in cemeteries?*
With great respect. One must not run there, nor speak without necessity, and if the weather permits, one ought not to walk there with one's head covered.

27. *Why is this so?*
Out of reverence for the crosses, for the bodies of Christians buried there, and because it is ground sanctified by the prayers of the Church.

28. *What is the episcopal residence?*
It is the palace of the bishop.

29. *What is the cloister?*
This name was often given to the set of buildings where the canons lived, who would only leave them to go to the church (this is what we call being "cloistered"). — The cloister sometimes also included the sacristy and the choir school for choir children, that is, the place where MASTERS instructed the choirboys.

30. *What is the presbytery?*
The presbytery (literally, "the house of the elders") is the residence of the parish priest, and sometimes of all the clergy attached to the parish.

31. *Why is it so called?*
Because, under the law of Jesus Christ as under

the law of Moses, the priests, by the grandeur of their functions, are as the Elders and the Wise of the people of God.

32. *What do you call cathedral churches?*

They are the churches in which there is a bishop.

33. *Why are they so called?*

This name derives from the Latin word *cathedra*, meaning "chair," because formerly only the bishop's church possessed a chair, the only place from which the Word of God was preached to the people. Today, there is in these churches a permanent throne for the bishop, called the EPIS-COPAL CHAIR.

34. *What do you call a Collegiate church?*

A church is so called when it is served by canons who chant the Office there daily. Collegiate comes from the word *collegium*, meaning "an assembly of several persons." Such were, in our country, the church of the former Abbey of Saint-Denis in France, the church of Sainte-Geneviève in Paris, and such still is the church of Notre-Dame de Fourvière in Lyons.

35. *What is a parish church?*

It is a church that has neither bishop nor canons, but is served by one or more priests for the care of the parish depending on it. If the bishop resides within that parish, it is at once a parish church and a cathedral.

36. *What do you call an oratory?*

This name is ordinarily given to a small chapel set apart solely for private prayer, where the Holy Mass is not celebrated.[3]

37. *What do you call the sanctuary in a church?*

The sanctuary is the most sacred part of a church. It is the place where the High Altar stands, and where the most holy functions of Christian worship take place, such as the Holy Sacrifice of the Mass and the exposition of the Most Blessed Sacrament. — It is the domain of the ministers of the altar. One also sees there, on the Gospel side[4] in cathedrals, the bishop's throne.

38. *What is the choir?*[5]

It is the area nearest the sanctuary where, during the Office, the priests, clerics, cantors, and altar boys take their place; in a word, all those who, by right of their order or by privilege, fulfill some role in the ceremonies of the Church.

39. *What are the chapels often found in great number in certain churches?*

They are the many small sanctuaries placed under the invocation of some Saint, where the

---

[3] According to current usage: "By the term oratory is understood a place for divine worship designated by permission of the ordinary for the benefit of some community or group of the faithful who gather in it and to which other members of the faithful can also come with the consent of the competent superior." *Code of Canon Law* [CIC] (1983), can. 1223.

[4] That is, the viewer's left when looking at the high altar.

[5] "Choir" here is used as a technical architectural term referring to a part of the church, not in the broader and more familiar sense of any body of singers, regardless of where they are singing in the church building.

Holy Sacrifice may be celebrated when needed, and where confessionals are most often situated.

40. *Is there a chapel more important than the others?*
Yes, it is the chapel of the Blessed Virgin.

41. *Why has an altar been raised in honor of Mary in every church?*
Because the Blessed Virgin is the Mother of all Christians, and after Jesus Christ, there is nothing in Heaven or on earth dearer to us than this good Mother.

42. *What is the nave?*
The nave is the part of the church which extends from the main entrance to the threshold of the choir.

43. *What are the aisles?*
In large churches, the term is given to the side naves which run alongside the main nave. All the faithful may take their place there as in the central nave. (It is worth noting that formerly one side of the church was reserved for men and the other for women; this laudable custom is still observed in several parishes.)

44. *What is the forecourt or portal?*
This name is given to the main entrance of a church. — It is there that, whenever possible the ceremonies preceding baptism are performed for children, that the new fire is blessed on Holy Saturday, and that a bishop or sovereign is received and welcomed when visiting a city.

45. *What is the bell tower?*

It is the tower in which the bells are enclosed.

46. *What then are the bells?*

The bells are instruments of metal which the Church employs to summon the faithful to her offices and ceremonies.

47. *Ought one to show respect to the bells?*

Yes, for the Church, having destined them to summon her children to the holy place, has separated them from profane things by a special blessing and even by a solemn consecration reserved to the bishop.

48. *What name is given to the blessing of the bells?*

It is commonly called the **BAPTISM OF BELLS**, doubtless because the bell is washed with holy water, anointed with holy oils, and given one or more names, whence also comes the custom of assigning to it a godfather and godmother. — However, the proper name of the ceremony is that of *Blessing*.

49. *How ought a Christian to regard the bell?*

As the voice of God and of the Church; it recalls his duties by calling him to prayer, it reminds him of his exile upon earth by announcing death or the funeral of one of his brethren; but it likewise brings to mind Christian joys: his baptism, his first communion, the visit of his bishop, and, in a word, all the solemn moments of his life.

§ III.
OF THE FURNISHINGS OF CHURCHES

50. *What is, among the furnishings of the church, the most venerable object?*

It is the altar.

51. *What do you mean by that name?*

Is it the name given to the table upon which the Holy Sacrifice is offered each day.

52. *What is the shape of the altar?*

Sometimes it takes the shape of a table supported by columns; but most often it has the shape of a tomb, for in former times the Holy Sacrifice was offered upon the tombs of the martyrs.

53. *What has the Church retained of this custom?*

The practice of placing relics of the saints within the altar-stone. — The place where these relics are enclosed is called the sepulcher.

54. *What is a fixed altar?*

It is a large stone table set in place, with or without masonry, and it loses its consecration if it is moved.[6] — Such an altar must be consecrated on site by a bishop.

55. *What is a portable altar?*

It is a smaller altar or a consecrated stone just large enough to permit the celebration of the Holy Sacrifice, which is set into an altar made of wood

---

[6] Current practice: "Sacred places [and altars] lose their dedication or blessing if they have been destroyed in large part, or have been turned over permanently to profane use by decree of the competent ordinary or in fact." CIC (1983), can. 1212.

or some other material. — These stones may be moved without losing their consecration.

56. *May anyone touch the altar-stone?*

No, only clerics in sacred orders may do so, because these stones have been consecrated and not merely blessed.

57. *Is the altar elevated?*

Yes, it must be raised by at least three steps above the nave, so that the faithful may see the priest at the altar and unite themselves to his prayers and to the ceremonies of the holy Mass.

58. *What are the accessories of the altar?*

They are: the **TABERNACLE**, the **CROSS**, the **CANDLESTICKS**, the **LAMPS**, the **ALTAR CLOTHS**, and the **COMMUNION RAIL**.

59. *What is the tabernacle?*

The tabernacle, according to the meaning of the word, is a small tent or pavilion placed in the center and at the rear of the altar, and serving solely to contain the Holy Eucharist.

60. *How ought the tabernacle to be constructed?*

The current rules of ecclesiastical discipline [7] require that it be made of marble, wood, or gilt bronze on the outside, and moreover covered with a white veil and lined within with white silk fabric, for white is the color used for all that pertains to the Blessed Sacrament. — It is worth noting here that all, both clergy and laity alike,

---

[7] At the time of this book's original publication.

must genuflect when passing before the tabernacle wherein the Holy Eucharist dwells.

61. *What is the Church's intention in all these regulations?*

It is to manifest her profound veneration for the Most Blessed Sacrament of the altar, which cannot be safeguarded with too great a reverence.

62. *What do you have to tell us about the throne of Eucharistic exposition?*[8]

It is a small throne of white silk, or a little niche of wood or gilt bronze, which is placed upon the tabernacle when the Blessed Sacrament is to be exposed for the adoration of the faithful. This throne may be used solely for the exposition of the Blessed Sacrament, and never for relics, not even those of the True Cross.

63. *Is the tabernacle an essential part of the altar?*

No, and indeed there ought to be but one in each church, at the high altar, or at most two, that is, one at the high altar and another in the particular chapel where the Holy Eucharist is reserved.

64. *Since we are on this point, where ought the Blessed Sacrament to be reserved?*

In smaller churches, it is more fitting that it be at the high altar, since this is ordinarily the most beautiful and the most worthy; but in cathedrals, it is preferable that it be kept in a private chapel, so that the order of the ceremonies may not be disturbed, and also because, during certain functions,

---

[8] Also called a thabor.

the bishop must be seated with his back turned to the altar, something which would be unbecoming were the Blessed Sacrament present there.

65. *By what sign would you recognize in a church the altar where the Blessed Sacrament is reserved?*

By the lamps, or at the very least by one lamp, which must burn there both day and night.

66. *How ought this lamp to be placed?*

If there be but one lamp, it ought to be placed in front of the altar, and not to the side, so that it may appear as a sentinel of honor stationed at the palace gate of the King of kings.

67. *What does this lamp signify?*

It expresses the ardor of our faith and of our love for Jesus Christ, and the desire we ought to have to keep watch, day and night, near His tabernacle.

68. *What are the other accessories of the altar?*

They are the crucifix and the candlesticks.

69. *How ought this crucifix to be?*

It ought to be placed at the center of the altar, or upon the tabernacle if there be one, and of sufficient size as to be visible to all the people. It must be a crucifix, and not merely a cross.

70. *What is the difference between a cross and a crucifix?*

The cross represents only the image of the sacred wood of our salvation, whereas the crucifix is the cross bearing the image of Our Lord crucified.

71. *Why does the Church desire that a crucifix be placed upon the altar?*

To remind us that it is by the sacrifice of the Cross, which is renewed upon the altar, that Jesus Christ has redeemed us.

72. *Whence comes the Church's use of candles and lamps?*

This usage dates back to the earliest days of Christianity. Lights were employed not only out of necessity, but also to honor our sacred mysteries and to remind the faithful, as the holy doctors teach us, that they must always show themselves to be true disciples of Him who was "the Light of the world."

73. *Why are there candlesticks with candles beside the cross on the altar?*

For the honor and veneration of the adorable sacrifice.

74. *What is their usual number?*

They must be six in number, and a seventh is to be added behind the cross when the bishop pontifically officiates, to signify, doubtless, the fullness of the priesthood which he received in his episcopal consecration.

75. *Of what material must the candles be made?*

Of beeswax, and never of stearine.[9]

---

[9] "Stearine" (from the Greek word *stear*, meaning "tallow" or "fat") is a hard, waxy substance derived from animal fat or vegetable oils. In the nineteenth century, it became a common ingredient in industrial candles because it was cheaper and more durable than beeswax.

76. *What is to be burned in the lamps?*
Oil.

77. *What is the reason for this choice of the Church?*
It lies in the nature and the symbolism of these two materials. Wax, drawn from the honey of bees, and oil, pressed from the olive, are two precious substances which the Church has deemed worthy of use in her worship. WAX, by its whiteness and the brilliance of its light, signifies the purity and charity which ought to adorn our hearts; and OIL, the strength and gentleness of the true Christian.

78. *What are torches or flambeaux?*
This name is given to large candles with three or four wicks, which are carried near the Blessed Sacrament during processions and at the moment of the Elevation or the Benediction of the Blessed Sacrament.

79. *What is the purpose of chandeliers and candelabra?*
They are used to support a greater number of candles which are lit during solemn feasts. By this, the Church seeks to manifest her joy and to stir us to greater fervor; such is the aim of all the solemnities of our holy religion.

80. *What do you call the communion rail?*
This name is given to the balustrade which ordinarily encloses the sanctuary and before which the faithful kneel to receive Holy Communion.

81. *Are there other particular objects in the sanctuary and at the high altar?*

Yes, for the public office: the credence, the bench of the sacred ministers, the bishop's throne (where applicable), and the Paschal candlestick during Eastertide.

82. *What is the credence?*

It is a table placed on the right-hand side within the sanctuary for the service of the altar during the Holy Sacrifice.

83. *Can you give us some details about the credence?*

The credence must be entirely covered with a white hanging cloth; upon it are placed all the objects necessary for a solemn Mass: the chalice fully prepared, the missal for the Gospel, the cruets, the thurible, the pax-brede, and at either end, the acolytes' candlesticks with their candles. If the office is pontifical, the miters, the vessels of holy oils, and all objects needed during the function are likewise placed there. The credence may be regarded as the sacristy of the sanctuary. It is near this credence that the acolytes remain throughout the Mass, so as to be ready to serve the sacred ministers.

84. *What is the ministers' bench?*[10]

It is a wooden bench covered with a cloth of the same color as the vestments, upon which the celebrant, the deacon, and the subdeacon sit, when appropriate, during Mass or Vespers. It ought to be situated on the right side of the altar and placed upon a carpet, without any step.

---

[10] Also called a sedilia.

85. *Of what does the bishop's throne consist and where is it placed?*

This throne is an armchair raised upon three steps and surmounted by draperies. It is required when a bishop officiates pontifically, and is placed on the Gospel side.

86. *What is the Paschal candlestick?*

It is a large candlestick placed on the floor of the sanctuary on the Gospel side, to support the Paschal candle from Holy Saturday until Ascension Day.

87. *What is the pulpit?*

It is a small tribune usually located in the middle of the great nave. From the pulpit, so as to be better heard by all, the priests announce to the faithful the fasts, feasts, and ceremonies of each week, read the Gospel, and finally deliver their instructions.

88. *What is the baptismal font?*

This name is given to a small basin, most often situated in a separate chapel. It contains the holy water for baptism, and it is at the font that this sacrament is administered.[11]

89. *Is there not within the font something called the piscina?*

Yes, it is a basin dug into the ground, into which falls, through a small hole in the font, the

---

[11] Traditionally, baptismal water (Easter water mixed with the oil of the catechumens and chrism oil) was created and blessed in the font during the Easter and Pentecost Vigils. Afterwards the water would be stored in the font itself. Nowadays, it is common to store baptismal water in a refrigerator.

water that has been poured upon the head of the child. Into it is also poured the water used to wash the sacred linens, when there is no other piscina in the church reserved for that purpose.

90. *What is a confessional?*

This is the name given to the sacred tribunal of penance, because it is there that one goes to CONFESS one's sins.

91. *What are the stalls?*

The term STALLS refers to the separate seats arranged in one or more rows on either side of the choir of the church.

92. *What is meant by the churchwardens' bench?*

It is a seat of honor where the churchwardens of the parish sit. — The clergy also sit there during the sermon, for this bench nearly always faces the pulpit.

93. *What is the organ?*

This name is given to a more or less complex apparatus of harmonious pipes, animated by compressed air and governed, by means of a keyboard, by the hand of a musician.

94. *What observation can one make concerning this admirable instrument?*

That it is proper to churches, and that the waves of harmony it pours forth in the holy place ought to recall to us, by their brilliance and solemnity, the chants so majestic, so sweet, and so full of delight which the angels and the blessed cause to be heard before the throne of the Eternal.

§ IV.
OF SACRED VESSELS AND UTENSILS

95. *What are the liturgical or sacred vessels?*

They are: the CHALICE, the PATEN, the CIBORIUM, the PYX, and the MONSTRANCE.

96. *What is the Chalice?*

It is a sacred vessel, namely the cup in which the wine is consecrated and changed into the Precious Blood of Our Lord in the Holy Sacrifice.

97. *What is the Paten?*

It is a kind of small plate used to hold the Sacred Host.

98. *What is the material of these two sacred vessels?*

According to the regulations of the Church, they must be of gold; or, if they are of silver, they must be gilded within.

99. *What is required in order that they may be used for the Holy Sacrifice?*

They must have been consecrated by the bishop.

100. *What is the Ciborium?*

The CIBORIUM is a vessel in which the Sacred Hosts are reserved for the Communion of the faithful. When it contains the sacred Species, it must be covered with a veil of white silk, or of cloth of gold or silver.

101. *What is the Custodia?*[12]

---

[12] Also called a luna, although this latter is more precisely a metal clip of sorts, in the shape of a crescent moon, which holds the Host.

It is a small case of gold or gilt silver, with double glass panes, in which the Sacred Host is enclosed, so that it may be placed within the Monstrance without fear of its being broken. Its Latin name, *custodia*, is derived from the verb *custodire*, which means "to guard."

102. *What is the Monstrance?*

The MONSTRANCE, whose name derives from the Latin word meaning "to show" (*monstrare*), is a vessel, or rather, a sacred implement, used to expose visibly the Sacred Host for the adoration of the faithful. – It is also called the Ostensorium.

103. *Are the Ciborium, the Pyx, and the Monstrance consecrated?*

No, they are only blessed by the bishop or by a priest who has received such faculty from the bishop.

104. *Is it permitted for the faithful to touch these vessels, even when the Body of Jesus Christ is not contained therein?*

No, only ecclesiastics have the right to do so.

105. *Do not the sacristans handle them in order to prepare them?*

No, unless they have received the express permission of the diocesan bishop, and that for their own parish only. But such practice is not in keeping with the spirit of the Roman Church, and in many dioceses this permission is granted only with great reluctance, and even then is strictly limited to the duties of the sacristy.

106. *Is it a sin to touch them without necessity?*
Yes, assuredly.

107. *What is meant by the term ampulla?*
They are the small vessels which contain the holy oils.

108. *May the faithful touch them?*
No, especially when they contain the consecrated oils.

109. *What are the principal objects, after the sacred vessels, used in the ceremonies of the Church?*
They are: the **CRUETS**, the **PAX-BREDE** or **PAX BOARD**, the **PROCESSIONAL CROSS**, the **THURIBLE**, the **BOAT** (for incense), the **HOLY WATER STOUPS**, the **ASPERGILLUM**, the **CANOPIES**, and the **BANNERS**.

110. *What are the cruets?*
They are small vessels of crystal or metal, in which are placed the water and wine for the Mass. They are set upon the credence on a tray of the same material.

111. *What is the pax-brede or pax board?*
It is a metal object upon which a crucifix is engraved, and which is presented to be kissed in order to bestow the sign of peace upon the faithful.

112. *What is the processional cross?*
It is a cross of considerable height which is carried in processions.

113. *What is the thurible?*

It is a small censer suspended by chains and intended to burn incense before the Blessed Sacrament or during the various ceremonies of the Church.

114. *What is the boat?*

It is a small vessel of metal in the form of a ship, hence its name, which serves to contain the incense that is burned in the thurible.

115. *What are the holy water stoups?*

They are vessels that contain the holy water.

116. *Are there various kinds?*

Yes, there is the stoup which is carried in the ceremonies of the Church, it is a vessel with a handle; and there are the urns or shells placed at the entrance of the church or the sacristy, for the use of the clergy and the faithful.

117. *What is the aspergillum?*

It is a small handle of wood or metal, to which bristles or a sponge are affixed, with which the priest sprinkles the faithful or the objects he blesses.

118. *What is the canopy?*

It is a pavilion of white silk which several persons hold aloft above the head of the priest in processions where the Blessed Sacrament is carried. The honors of the canopy are also accorded to bishops and sovereigns; but in the latter case, it ought, as far as possible, to be red or violet.

119. *What is the umbraculum or ombrellino?*

It is a smaller canopy, which may be carried by a single person. It is used when the Blessed Sacrament is carried to the sick, or conveyed within the church.

120. *What are the banners?*

They are standards or flags of cloth upon which are depicted images of the Blessed Virgin, the patron saint of the parish, or of the various confraternities which bear them in procession.

§ V.
OF THE SACRED LINENS

121. *What are the sacred linens used in the Holy Sacrifice?*

They are: the **CORPORAL**, the **PALL**, the **PURIFICATOR**, the **MANUTERGE**, and the **ALTAR CLOTHS**, to which may be added the **COMMUNION CLOTH**.

122. *What is the corporal?*

The corporal is a small and very fine linen cloth, without embroidery, which is placed upon the other cloths of the altar, to receive thereon the Body of Our Lord during the Holy Sacrifice, hence its name *corporal*.[13] It is also always upon the corporal that the sacred vessels must be placed when they contain the Holy Eucharist.

123. *What is the pall?*

It is a corporal folded into a square or stiffened

---

[13] From the Latin word for "body," *corpus.*

with a small piece of cardboard,[14] which serves to cover the chalice during the Holy Mass.

124. *What is the purificator?*

It is a small linen cloth used by the priest to wipe the chalice, his lips, and his fingers after the communion of the Precious Blood and the ablutions.

125. *May the laity touch these linens?*

No, they may not, once these linens have been used even once in the Holy Sacrifice.

126. *How are these linens to be washed?*

A priest, or a person having the right or permission to handle sacred vessels,[15] purifies them in three separate waters, which are then poured into the *piscina*. Only after these precautions may they be entrusted to the hands of ordinary laundresses.

127. *What is the manuterge?*

The manuterge, or LAVABO TOWEL, is the hand towel the priest uses at the altar when he washes his fingers.

128. *What are the altar cloths?*

They are linens with which the Church prescribes the altar be covered in order to celebrate

---

[14] It is not clear that anyone does this anymore; for a long time, palls have been made as separately dedicated items. Historically the pall developed from the corporal: originally the chalice was covered by pulling part of the rather large corporal over it, and the Ritual has the same blessing for palls and corporals, pointing to their kinship.

[15] Even in the 1917 Code of Canon Law (can. 1306), one had to be a subdeacon to purify the linens. This task is expressly noted in the ordination rite for the subdiaconate.

upon it the Holy Sacrifice of the Mass. There must be three, and the uppermost ought to hang down almost to the ground at both ends of the altar.

129. *What is the communion cloth?*

It is a linen cloth spread upon the sanctuary rail, or held out by clerics to the faithful during the reception of Holy Communion.

130. *May the faithful touch the manuterge or the communion cloths?*

Nothing forbids it, since these cloths are never in contact with the Body of Our Lord Jesus Christ. The same holds true for the altar cloths.

131. *Of what material must all these linens be made?*

The rules of the Church prescribe that they be made of linen or hempen cloth.[16]

---

[16] On an historical and symbolic level, recall that Our Lord's Body was wrapped in linen while in the tomb. On a practical level, linen absorbs liquid well.

CHAPTER II

✠

Of the Sacred Vestments

§ I.
THE VESTURES OF ECCLESIASTICS, – CHOIR HABITS, – THE VESTMENTS OF THE SACRED MINISTERS

132. *What is the cassock?*

The cassock is a long robe descending to the heels. It is the vesture of all ecclesiastics.

133. *What is the color of the cassock?*

It varies according to the dignity of him who wears it: the pope wears white; the cardinals, red; the bishops, violet; and simple priests, black, as do all ecclesiastics of lower rank. It is often accompanied, especially in France, by a cincture of the same color.

134. *Do ecclesiastics wear it exclusively?*

Yes, ordinarily; but laymen are permitted to wear it within the church when they form part of the lower choir. Seminarians who are not yet tonsured[1] are likewise authorized to wear it even outside the church.

135. *How ought the cantors and altar boys of churches to make use of this permission?*

They ought to regard it as a great honor and to treat this sacred habit with reverence.

---

[1] See no. 674.

136. *What does the cassock signify?*

It signifies renunciation of the world.

137. *What is the surplice?*

The surplice, so called because it was formerly worn *over* a fur-lined garment or cassock for winter, is a white vestment descending to the knees, with sleeves that cover the entire arm and are at the same time very wide.

138. *What does the surplice signify?*

By its whiteness, it signifies the innocence that those who approach the holy mysteries ought to bring to the altar.

139. *What is the rochet?*

It is a shorter surplice with narrow sleeves, and is the ordinary choir vesture of bishops, secular prelates, and canons.

140. *What is the biretta?*

The biretta is a black cap with three or four peaks, used by ecclesiastics and even by clerics of the lower choir to cover the head during Offices or in processions.

141. *What is the camail?*

It is a small mantle or shoulder-cape, ordinarily of the same color as the cassock, accompanied by a hood, and used in winter. — The MOZZETTA, which is worn in all seasons by canons and bishops and is a mark of dignity, is nothing other than a small camail.

142. *What do you know of the canons' cappa?*

This cappa, in Latin *cappa magna* or "great cape," is composed of a camail of silk or ermine and a long silk mantle with a trailing train, the color of which varies. The pope and cardinals wear a red cappa; bishops wear violet; as for the canons, the color of this mantle varies according to the customs or privileges of the chapters to which they belong. Most often, it is of black cloth trimmed with red; but this vesture is not the true CAPPA MAGNA.

143. *Is this garb of the canons in general use?*

It is scarcely known save in certain dioceses of France. Their true vesture is the rochet and mozzetta, and at times the almuce.[2]

144. *What are the vestments common to clerics in sacred orders?*

They are: the AMICE, the ALB, and the CINCTURE.

145. *What is the amice?*

It is a linen veil with which the ministers of the altar wrap around the neck when they are to vest in the alb.

146. *What does the amice signify?*

As it was formerly worn upon the head, the Church has made of it the image of the "helmet of salvation" with which Saint Paul would have every Christian be armed. This is why the priest, before letting the amice fall upon his shoulders, places it on his head while saying: "Place upon thy head, O Lord, the helmet of salvation."

---

[2] The almuce is a hoodlike shoulder cape.

147. *What is the alb?*

The alb is a white garment, as its name (*alba*) indicates, which descends down to the feet, and in which the priests and ministers of the altar must be vested.

148. *What does the alb signify?*

It signifies innocence, which is as it were the vesture of the priest, and which casts a radiance over the whole of his life, as the whiteness of the alb casts a brightness over the whole of the body which it entirely envelops.

149. *What is the cincture?*

It is a girdle which holds the folds of the alb about the loins. It signifies modesty and good morals.

150. *What is the proper vestment of the subdeacon and of the higher orders?*

It is the maniple, which lower clerics are not permitted to wear.

151. *What is the maniple?*

It is a small silk ornament, like all sacred vestments we are to speak of, worn upon the left arm by ministers of the altar during the Holy Sacrifice. Formerly, it was a cloth carried by clerics to wipe away sweat when it troubled them, or the tears that devotion drew from their eyes.

152. *What meaning has been attributed to it since it became an ornament?*

It signifies the tears of the Christian upon earth, and reminds the priest that he must weep

many a tear and shed many a sweat for the salvation of souls, if he would be rewarded by God
in Heaven.

153. *What is the other ornament of the subdeacon?*

It is the tunicle, which was formerly a rather
long robe. Today it is shorter, and in France,
where the sleeves have been cut beneath the arms,
it has become a sort of mantle.

154. *What does the tunicle signify?*

It signifies the joy the subdeacon ought to feel
in having consecrated his life to the service of
God.

**155. *Is there not another ornament proper to the
subdeacon?***

Yes, it is the HUMERAL, or veil of silk, of the
same color as the vestments, which is laid upon
his shoulders when he is to carry the chalice to
the altar and the paten after the Offertory, in
solemn Masses.

156. *What are the vestments of the deacon?*

The same as those of the inferior orders, and
moreover, the stole and the dalmatic.

157. *What is the stole?*

It is an ornament in the form of a band which
the deacon wears across the body, passing it from
the left shoulder beneath the right arm.

158. *Why is it worn in that manner?*

Because formerly the stole was a robe, of which
only the border or facing has been retained, and

the deacon, to be free to assist the priest at the altar, would disengage the right sleeve and fasten it beneath the arm.

159. *What does the stole signify?*

The Church has made it the symbol or image of the garment of immortality which was restored to us in baptism.

160. *What is the dalmatic?*

It was formerly a robe quite similar to the tunicle of today. Now they differ not at all, though each has retained its name.

161. *What does the dalmatic signify?*

The justice which every minister of the altar ought to carry into his functions.

162. *What are the particular vestments of the priest?*

They are the maniple, of which we have spoken about above, the stole, and the chasuble.

163. *Does the priest wear the stole as the deacons do?*

No, he wears it hanging down in front, to signify that he bears the full weight of the priesthood, or crossed over the breast when putting it on over the alb.

164. *What is the chasuble?*

The chasuble is the sacred garment which the priest puts on over all the others to celebrate the Holy Mass. This vestment bears a large cross over the entire portion that covers the priest's shoulders. In Italy, the cross of the chasuble is on the front.

165. *What does the chasuble signify?*

It signifies the yoke of the law of Jesus Christ, which the priest bears upon himself, to teach the faithful to take it up willingly for the salvation of their souls.

166. *Do you know of other vestments in ordinary use during the sacred offices?*

Yes, there are also the cope and the humeral veil.

167. *What is the cope?*

The cope, or PLUVIAL, which differs from the grand cope of bishops and canons described in number 142, is a large mantle of silk worn by the priest during processions and on certain solemn occasions. It is generally not assigned any particular mystical meaning, but its majestic form is undoubtedly the reason for its use in the solemn circumstances of the liturgy.

168. *What is the scarf or humeral veil?*

The scarf or HUMERAL VEIL is a white silk veil placed upon the priest's shoulders and wrapped around his hands to give the blessing with the Blessed Sacrament or to carry It in procession.

169. *Why is this veil used?*

To manifest the profound reverence owed to the sacred vessels, and above all to the adorable Body of Our Lord, which is to be touched with bare hands as little as possible.

170. *Are all the ornaments of the Church of the same color?*

No, the Church employs five different colors: white, red, green, violet, and black.

171. *What do these colors signify?*

WHITE signifies joy and purity; RED, the love of God and the courage to shed our blood for Him; GREEN, hope and the repose of the life to come; VIOLET, penance and prayer amid affliction; and BLACK, mourning and sorrow.

172. *Tell us briefly how these colors are generally used.*

WHITE is used for all the feasts of Our Lord, of the Blessed Virgin, and of all saints who are not martyrs; RED, for the feasts and offices of the Holy Ghost, for the feasts of the Cross and the Passion, and for those of the Martyrs; GREEN, for the season of pilgrimage (that is, the Sundays after Epiphany and after Pentecost), and on the ferial days of that season; VIOLET, for all Sundays of Advent, Septuagesima, and Lent, as well as for all offices of penance; and finally, BLACK, for Good Friday during the morning office,[3] and for all offices of the dead.

173. *Are the Church's vestments, linens, and ornaments all blessed?*

All those which serve directly at the Holy Sacrifice of the altar must be so; moreover, it is a pious and praiseworthy custom to bless all objects used in divine worship.

---

[3] That is, the Mass of the Presanctified, which was at the time of this writing celebrated before noon.

174. *By whom must sacred linens and ornaments be blessed?*

By the bishop, or at least, by a priest who has received express permission from him.

§ II.
THE VESTURE AND PARTICULAR ORNAMENTS OF BISHOPS

175. *What is the customary attire of bishops in their private life?*

Bishops wear a violet cassock, a mantle, and violet stockings; a cincture of the same color adorned with a tassel of interwoven green and gold silk; and a black hat trimmed with a tassel made of the same material as that of the cincture. In certain countries, the violet garments of bishops are further embellished with red facings, borders, and buttons. Cardinals are vested in the same manner as bishops, save for the color of their garment, which is scarlet, and the tassels of their hat and cincture, which are wholly of gold or of gold interwoven with red.

176. *What are the sacred vestments of bishops?*

They are: the sandals and stockings, the pectoral cross, the tunicles, the gloves, the ring, the miter, the crozier (and, if he be an archbishop, the pallium and the cross).

177. *What are the stockings and the sandals?*

The stockings or buskins, made of silk and similar in form to those we ourselves wear, cover the bishop's legs up to the knees. The sandals are silk shoes, adorned with a cross embroidered in gold. These two ornaments must correspond in color to the liturgical ornaments of the day.

178. *Whence comes the usage of this footwear?*

Because the coarse footwear of our forebears was not deemed sufficiently decorous for the altar, priests were enjoined to wear more precious sandals when celebrating. Bishops, in later times, alone retained this usage for pontifical ceremonies.

179. *What is the pectoral cross?*

It is a cross of gold which the bishop always wears upon his breast. It is one of the insignia, and one might say the distinctive insignia, of the episcopate. The one the bishop uses to celebrate Holy Mass ought to contain relics, ordinarily of the True Cross and of the martyrs.

180. *What are the tunicles?*

This name is given to the tunicle and the dalmatic of silk, the vestments of the subdeacon and the deacon, which the bishop wears beneath the chasuble, according to the form they formerly (or nearly) possessed.

181. *What are the gloves?*

The gloves with which the bishop covers his hands are a mark of dignity. They may also signify reverence for holy things, of which the bishop must give example to his flock. This vestment likewise conforms to the liturgical color of the day and is adorned with a cross embroidered in gold.

182. *What does the ring which bishops wear represent?*

It represents the spiritual bond between the bishop and the church which he has been called to govern.

183. *What is the miter?*

It is the headpiece or crown of the bishop. It is made either of rich fabric embroidered with gold, or of linen. This latter, simpler miter is sometimes used on occasions that are, nonetheless, most solemn. In the mind of the Church, the miter is a vestment of glory and honor.

184. *What is the crozier?*

The crozier is an ornate staff made of gold, or gilt silver, or even of wood, upon which the bishop leans in the exercise of his sacred functions. The croziers of abbots of monasteries are most often made of wood or ivory.

185. *What does the crozier signify?*

The crozier is the emblem of the bishop's authority; it is as it were the scepter of his spiritual kingship. It is also his pastoral staff.

186. *What is the gremial?*

The gremial is the name given to a precious veil placed upon the bishop's knees when he is seated. Formerly, it was not regarded as a vestment but was merely a white linen cloth presented to the bishop, and even to the priest, when seated, so that by resting their hands upon it, they might not soil the sacred ornaments.

187. *What is the distinctive ornament of an arch-bishop?*

It is the pallium.

188. *What is the pallium?*

The pallium consists of a band of white wool adorned with several black silk crosses. To this band, which encircles the shoulders, are attached two pendants: one falling upon the breast, the other down the back. As it is worn today, the pallium is no longer, like the stole, anything more than the border or trimming of a mantle of honor formerly granted to the princes of the Church. In order to wear it, one must have received it from the pope, who blesses it on the feast of Saint Peter at the tomb of that great Apostle. It is a privilege the pope sometimes grants to a bishop; but it is a singular and very rare favor.

189. *What other mark of distinction do archbish-ops possess?*

They also have the right to have carried before them their archiepiscopal cross, the face of the crucifix being turned toward the archbishop. This cross may precede the archbishop only within his province or in the presence of a papal legate.

190. *What is the distinctive insignia of the dignity of the cardinalate?*

It is the red hat. This hat, with wide brim and adorned with three tiers of tassels, is worn by cardinals only when vested in choir dress. Otherwise, they wear it in black or red, but smaller and with upturned brims in the form of a tricorne.

191. *What particular feature distinguishes the cassock of cardinals, bishops, and lesser prelates?*

Besides the particular color, which all substitute black during Lent, their cassock also has a long train, carried during ceremonies by one of their attendants. The cassock with a train is a privilege of the prelature, though often prelates wear the cassock without a train in the presence of their superiors or in ceremonies where they are not permitted to have it carried.[4]

<h2 style="text-align:center">§ III.
THE VESTURE AND PARTICULAR ORNAMENTS OF THE POPE</h2>

192. *How is the Holy Father attired in his private life?*

The pope is clothed in a cassock of white silk or wool; he also wears a white skullcap and red velvet shoes, the upper part of which is adorned with a cross embroidered in gold. This footwear is commonly called the pope's mules. When the pope goes out, he wears a red silk hat with a gold tassel, and in winter, a red mantle.

193. *Is it not customary to kiss the pope's mule when presenting oneself before him?*

Yes, and crowned heads themselves lower their majesty before the representative of Jesus Christ

---

[4] In 1952, Pius XII (1939–1958) abolished the use, by prelates, of cassocks with trains. Their appearance is first documented in the early eighteenth century, and their employment was merely a matter of custom, for they were never mentioned in the Ceremonial of Bishops.

on earth. One kisses the cross that is upon the Holy Father's mule.

194. *What is the pope's choir dress?*

His ordinary choir dress consists of white stockings, red shoes, the white cassock and skull-cap, a girdle with gold tassels, the lace rochet, the red mozzetta trimmed with ermine, and the stole.

195. *What is the falda?*

The falda is a wide robe of white silk with a trailing train which the Holy Father wears when he celebrates Mass himself or assists at the Office with great solemnity; it is worn over the cassock and beneath all the other ornaments. This long robe is carried by a high dignitary of the pontifical court.

196. *What particularity distinguishes the pope's cope?*

That it is trailing and fastened upon the chest by a broad clasp, called a "morse," of silver or vermeil adorned with engravings.

197. *Does the pope wear the miter?*

Yes, when he officiates; but at times, in place of the miter, he wears the tiara.

198. *What is the tiara?*

It is a miter adorned with three crowns placed one above the other.

199. *What do these three crowns signify?*

They remind the faithful of the triple power of the Vicar of Jesus Christ over the whole Church:

over the **CHURCH MILITANT**, which he governs here below; over the **CHURCH SUFFERING**, which he relieves through the dispensation of indulgences; and even over the **CHURCH TRIUMPHANT**, by the august privilege he holds of awarding the honors of public cult to the servants of God whose sanctity has been manifested by miracles.

200. *What is particular to the pope's ring?*

That it represents Saint Peter in his boat casting his nets into the sea; hence it is called the Ring of the Fisherman. At the death of the pope, this ring is broken.

201. *Does the pope carry the crozier?*

No, never.

202. *Why is this so?*

Pope Innocent III relates that Saint Peter, having sent his pastoral staff to Eucharius, first bishop of Trier, the inhabitants of that city would never consent to relinquish so precious a relic. It is further said that, for this reason, the popes make use of the crozier only within the churches of Trier.

203. *What is the* sedia gestatoria?

The *sedia gestatoria* is a throne upon which the Sovereign Pontiff is carried during great solemnities.

204. *Is the cross carried before the pope?*

Yes, and throughout the whole world, for his spiritual jurisdiction knows no boundaries upon the earth, any more than does the reign of Jesus Christ, of whom he is the representative.

✠

PRINCIPAL FUNCTIONS OF THE LITURGY

❦❦❦❦❦❦❦❦❦❦❦❦❦❦❦❦❦❦❦❦❦❦❦❦❦❦

CHAPTER I

✠

On the Holy Sacrifice of the Mass

§ I.
ON THE HOLY SACRIFICE IN GENERAL

205. *What is the Holy Sacrifice of the Mass?*

It is the most august of all liturgical functions; it is the Sacrifice of the Cross; it is the sacrifice of the Body and Blood of Jesus Christ renewed upon the altar under the appearances of bread and wine.

206. *Who are the ministers of this sacrifice?*

They are of two kinds: the sacred ministers and the inferior ministers.

207. *Who are the sacred ministers?*

They are: the celebrant, the deacon, and the subdeacon.

208. *Who are the inferior ministers?*

They are the acolytes, the thurifer, the master of ceremonies, and the cantors.

209. *What are the functions of the celebrant?*

His august functions are to consecrate the Body and Blood of Our Lord Jesus Christ, to pray aloud in the name of the whole faithful people, and to bless them in the name of God, whose representative he is at the holy altar.

210. *What are the functions of the deacon?*

The deacon, as his name signifies ("minister," "servant") is charged with serving the priest at the altar. He stands always at his side, or slightly behind, in order to be ready to assist him at every moment. He presents the bread, pours the wine into the chalice, and even recites with the priest the prayer of oblation over the chalice which begins with these words: *Offerimus tibi*, "We offer unto Thee, O Lord..." He sings the Gospel, and dismisses the people at the end of Mass with the singing of the *Ite missa est*.

211. *What are the functions of the subdeacon?*

The subdeacon performs at the Holy Sacrifice functions of lesser dignity than those of the deacon. He is rarely at the priest's side: he carries the chalice to the altar, adds the water at the Offertory, holds the paten from the Oblation until the *Pater noster*, and bears to the choir the kiss of peace which he has received from the deacon. It is likewise his office to chant the Epistle.

212. *What are the functions of the acolytes?*

The acolytes, whose name means "follower" or "servant," are as it were the attendants of the deacon and subdeacon. They bear the torches beside the cross in procession and before the ministers as they proceed to the altar; they present the water and wine to the deacon and subdeacon, and give the celebrant water for the washing of hands. For this reason their place is near the credence, so that they may always be ready to provide the ministers with all that is needful.

213. *What are the functions of the thurifer?*

The thurifer is a cleric who carries the incense and the thurible to the altar. He is charged with presenting them to the sacred ministers and with incensing the clerics not in holy orders,[1] as well as the people. He also incenses the Blessed Sacrament at the elevation and at benediction.

214. *What are the functions of the master of ceremonies?*

As his title suggests, he is charged with ensuring the good order of the ceremonies. It is also his duty (provided he is a tonsured cleric)[2] to assist the celebrant at the missal and to turn its pages.

215. *Who are the cantors?*

The cantors are clerics whose function is to respond to the chants of the priest and to support the singing of the faithful and the choir.

216. *Do laymen have the right to fulfill ecclesiastical functions at the Holy Sacrifice of the Mass?*

No, they have no such right. It is only by privilege and in the absence of true clerics that they are permitted to assume the functions of the inferior ministers themselves.

217. *Are all these ministers necessary for every Mass?*

No, they are required only for the solemn Mass; at low Mass one minister suffices. He is a cleric or a choir-boy and is called the ALTAR SERVER.

---

[1] It is more typical to see the deacon incensing those in choir while the thurifer incenses the clerics/servers not in choir.

[2] Nowadays, this function is commonly performed by the non-tonsured but with some ceremonial differences.

218. *In what spirit ought laymen to carry out the sacred functions of acolyte, thurifer, master of ceremonies, or altar server?*

In a spirit of deep faith, reverence, recollection, and even gratitude for the honor bestowed upon them in being permitted to approach so near to the altar.

219. *How many kinds of Mass are distinguished?*

Two kinds are distinguished: low or private Masses, and high or solemn Masses.

§ II.
OF THE LOW MASS

220. *What is a Low Mass?*

This name is given to those Masses celebrated without chant, and with only one server, or two at most.

221. *What preparations are necessary for the celebration of Holy Mass?*

A few moments before the hour of the Sacrifice, the altar being arranged as described above (numbers 50 to 76), three altar cards, or **CANONS**, are placed upon it, upon which certain prayers of the Mass are written; as well as a cushion or a stand for the missal. The cleric, having washed his hands and vested in his choir habit (cassock and surplice),[3] sets out the cruets upon the credence,

---

[3] Although the original ceremonial rubrics of Tridentine Roman Missal did prescribe wearing the surplice beneath the other priestly vestments "if it can be done conveniently," Adrian Fortescue observed in 1917 that the practice was seldom observed in England. The 1960 rubrics promulgated by John XXIII (1958–1963) removed this requirement.

lights two candles, and, returning to the sacristy, takes up the missal, which he reverently carries resting against his breast.[4] When the hour of Mass has come, the priest, preceded by the cleric, proceeds to the altar.

222. *What does this procession of the priest to the altar represent?*

It represents Jesus Christ going up to Jerusalem to endure there the sufferings of His Passion.

223. *What do you call the first part of the Mass?*
The Preparation.

224. *What does it contain?*

It contains the priest's prayers at the foot of the altar: the INTROIT, the KYRIE, the GLORIA IN EXCELSIS, and the COLLECT.

225. *Why does the priest, at the beginning of the Mass, pray at the foot of the altar?*

He does so in a spirit of humility, praying and confessing his sins at the foot of the altar before ascending it for the awe-inspiring ministry entrusted to him.

226. *What does the altar represent?*

The altar represents Jesus Christ; for this reason the priest often kisses it with reverence.

---

[4] According to the original rubrics of the Tridentine Roman Missal, the server was to bring the missal from the sacristy as he processed to the altar with the priest, and to take it back with him when he returned to the sacristy after Mass. Many places, however, adopted the custom of setting the missal on the altar before Mass, leaving it there at the end. The 1960 rubrics permit either practice.

227. *What thought ought one to have upon seeing the priest ascend the altar?*

One ought to call to mind Jesus Christ ascending Calvary.

228. *What is the Introit?*

The Introit, which means "entrance," is an antiphon followed by a verse from a psalm and the **GLORIA PATRI**, and is sung at the moment of the priest's entrance to the altar.

229. *What is the* Kyrie eleison*?*

It is a prayer in the Greek tongue in which we beg each of the three Persons of the Most Holy Trinity three times to have mercy upon us. The first three *Kyries* are addressed to the Father, the next three [*Christes*] to the Son, and the final three [*Kyries*] to the Holy Ghost.

230. *What is the* Gloria in excelsis*?*

It is the song of the angels at the birth of Our Lord Jesus Christ, a hymn of joy in honor of the Most Holy Trinity.

231. *Is it said at every Mass?*

It is said on all Sundays of the year, on all feasts, and throughout the Paschal season, which is a time of joy for Christians; but it is omitted at Masses during Advent and Lent, at votive Masses, penitential Masses, and Masses for the dead.

232. *What is the meaning of* Dominus vobiscum, *which the priest so often says during the Holy Mass?*

It is a salutation of peace which the priest gives to the faithful. As a sign of that peace, before saying the *Dominus vobiscum*, he kisses the altar to show that it is the peace of Jesus Christ Himself which he imparts to the Christian people in saying: "The Lord be with you." The response is: *Et cum spiritu tuo*: "And with thy spirit."

233. *What is the* Collect*?*

This is the name given to the first prayer of the Mass. It is so called because in it the priest prays for the whole assembly (*collectio*) of the faithful gathered to assist at the Holy Sacrifice. There are sometimes several Collects.[5]

234. *What do you call the second part of the Mass?*
The INSTRUCTION.

235. *What does it contain?*
The EPISTLE, the GRADUAL, the ALLELUIA, and sometimes the TRACT and the PROSE or SEQUENCE, the GOSPEL, and the CREED (*Credo*) or SYMBOL.

236. *What is the Epistle?*
It is a passage, more or less lengthy, taken from Holy Scripture and read by the priest after the Collect. This passage is ordinarily taken from the New Testament, especially from the letters or Epistles of the Apostles, hence its name.

237. *Why does one answer* Deo gratias *[Thanks be to God] at the end?*

---

[5] In the original Tridentine Missal, having several Collects was the norm outside of the most solemn feasts. The total number depended on the day's liturgical rank, and a maximum of seven could be said. The 1960 rubrics promulgated by John XXIII drastically reduced the cases where multiple collects are to be said, and set the maximum at three.

To thank God for having deigned to speak to us through His apostles and prophets.

238. *What is the Gradual?*

It is a verse from the psalms sung after the Epistle. It is called the GRADUAL because in former times it was sung upon the steps of the ambo, a kind of elevated lectern (from the Latin *gradus*, "step").

239. *What is the Alleluia?*

It is a cry of joy, borrowed from the Hebrew tongue, which is sung after the Gradual. It is followed by a verse from Holy Scripture. During penitential days, the ALLELUIA is replaced by the TRACT, a rather rapid but mournful chant composed of several verses of Scripture.

240. *What is the Prose?*

It is a rhymed hymn sung after the verse of the ALLELUIA on certain feast days.

241. *What is the origin of the Proses?*

Formerly, a series of words was added to the neume of the ALLELUIA, and this was called a Sequence, or continuation of the ALLELUIA. These words, being rhymed but not metrical like verses, were later given the name we still use: PROSES. However, the Missal retains for them the Latin name *sequentia*.

242. *Why does the priest pray in deep inclination in the middle of the altar before the Gospel?*

In order to ask God, by a particular prayer, to purify his heart so that he may worthily proclaim His holy Gospel.

243. *What is the Gospel?*

The Gospel at Mass is a passage taken from one of the four Evangelists who wrote the life and words of Our Lord.

244. *How ought one to listen to the Gospel?*

Always standing.

245. *Why is this so?*

Out of reverence for the word of God, and to show that we are ready to follow Jesus Christ and to defend the faith taught to us in the Gospel.

246. *Why do the priest and the faithful make the sign of the cross upon their forehead, lips, and breast at the beginning of the Gospel?*

To show that they are not ashamed of the Gospel of Jesus Christ,[6] and that they are disposed to proclaim with their lips the faith they hold in their hearts.

247. *Why does the priest kiss the Gospel when he has finished reading it?*

To show his reverence for that divine word, and to inspire the faithful with the same sentiments.

248. *What does the priest recite after the Gospel?*

He recites the CREED, which is a profession of faith and the summary of Catholic doctrine.

249. *Is it always recited?*

No, only on Sundays and on the more solemn feast days when the faithful assist in greater

---

[6] As shame manifests itself through the forehead: see St. Thomas Aquinas, *Summa theologiae* III, Q. 72, art. 9.

number at the Holy Sacrifice, and also on the feasts of the Apostles and Doctors,[7] because they devoted their lives and their learning to the defense of the truths contained in the Creed.

250. *Why do we genuflect at the words:* Et incarnatus est *[And was incarnate]?*

To testify to our faith in the mystery of the Incarnation, and to express our love and gratitude toward the Savior of our souls.

251. *What name is given to the next part of the Mass?*

It is called the OBLATION.

252. *What does this part include?*

It includes the offering of the bread, the preparation of the wine and water in the chalice, the oblation of the chalice, the washing of the hands, the *Orate fratres*, and the Secret.

253. *Why does the priest put a little water into the wine which he is to consecrate?*

To represent human nature united to the divinity in the person of Our Lord, and also the water which flowed with blood from His side upon the Cross.

254. *Why does the priest wash his hands, and why does he wash them away from the altar?*

The priest washes his hands to show the great purity with which one must approach the holy mysteries; and he does so away from the altar out of reverence, for the washing of the hands is

---

[7] The recitation of the Creed on feasts of Doctors was suppressed in 1960.

at once a common action and an act of humility.

255. *Why does the priest again ask for the prayers of the faithful with the words* Orate fratres *[Pray, brethren]?*

He does this before entering into the solemn moment of the Consecration, so that the faithful may unite themselves more closely to the sacrifice he is about to offer in their name. From the *Orate fratres* until after Communion, he no longer turns toward the people.

256. *What do you call the* Secrets?

They are the prayers which the priest recites after the *Suscipiat* of the faithful. They are called SECRETS because the priest must recite them in a low voice.

257. *What is the fourth part of the Mass?*

It is the Canon, or the RULE OF CONSECRATION.

258. *What is the Preface?*

The Preface, or Introduction, is the solemn beginning of the Canon of the Mass. It ends with the song of the angels in Heaven: *Sanctus, Sanctus, Sanctus*; "Holy, holy, holy is the Lord," etc.

259. *What then is the Canon of the Mass?*

This name is given to the prayers that immediately precede, accompany, or follow the Consecration, up to the *Pater noster.* CANON means "rule"; thus all the prayers of the Canon are ordered in such a way that they never change.[8]

---

[8] John XXIII directed that the name of St. Joseph be added to the Canon in 1962.

260. *What is the first prayer of the Canon?*

It is the *Te igitur*, wherein the priest prays the Lord to be pleased with the gifts of the sacrifice, a prayer addressed to God in union with the pope, the bishop, and all the faithful.

261. *What is the second prayer?*

It is the *Memento*, or commemoration of the living. In this prayer the priest pauses for a moment to offer intercession for the living faithful for whom he offers the Holy Sacrifice, and for whom he must, or desires, to pray in a special manner.

262. *What is the third prayer?*

It is the prayer *Communicantes*, in which the priest implores the help of Heaven for himself and for the faithful people, beseeching it through the intercession of the Blessed Virgin Mary, of the holy Apostles, and of the martyrs, several of the most renowned among whom are named in this prayer.

263. *What is the fourth prayer?*

It is the prayer *Hanc igitur*, in which the priest, laying his hands upon the offerings of the sacrifice, beseeches that the Host he is about to offer may be for us a pledge of peace and salvation, and may preserve us from eternal damnation.

264. *At what moment does the change of the bread and wine into the Body and Blood of Our Lord Jesus Christ take place?*

It is at the moment when the priest, bowed over the altar and holding first the bread, then the wine, in his hands, pronounces the words which, by the will and omnipotence of Jesus Christ the Sovereign Priest, accomplish the great miracle of the Eucharist.

265. *Why does the priest elevate the Sacred Host and the Chalice after the consecration?*

To expose them to the adoration of the faithful present at the august Sacrifice; and to signal to the people to prostrate themselves, the bell is rung.

266. *Why is the chasuble of the priest lifted at this moment?*

Because in former times this was necessary on account of the ample form of the chasubles; this custom has been retained as a memorial of ancient usage.

267. *What is the fifth part of the Mass?*

It is the COMMUNION.

268. *Of what does this part of the Mass consist?*

It consists of the preparation for Communion and of Communion itself.

269. *What do to be noted with regard to the preparation for Communion?*

I note the *Pater noster*, the Fraction of the Host, the *Agnus Dei*, the three prayers before Communion, and the *Domine non sum dignus*.

270. *Why is the* Pater noster *recited?*

Because the Church has judged that no prayer is more worthy to be included than that which was taught by Our Lord Himself.

271. *How is the breaking of the bread performed, and what does it signify?*

The priest breaks the Sacred Host into three parts, after the example of Jesus Christ, who broke the bread changed into His Body to give it to His disciples. Then he mingles a portion of the consecrated Host with the Precious Blood in the chalice, to signify the Resurrection of the Savior, and also the union of His Body and Blood under each of the species separately present upon the altar.

272. *What is the* **Agnus Dei***?*

It is a prayer composed of the words of Saint John the Baptist, who pointed out Jesus Christ to the Jewish people as their Savior. It is repeated three times and is addressed to Jesus Christ, the Lamb of God, immolated for our salvation, to obtain mercy for our sins; which we also express by striking our breast at the words *Miserere nobis*, "have mercy on us."

273. *What have you to say of the three prayers before Communion?*

In the first, the priest asks for himself and for the Church the peace which Jesus promised to His Apostles; in the second, he prays to be delivered from all sin, that he may receive the adorable Sacrament more worthily; and in the third, he beseeches that the reception of the divine Eucharist may not turn to his condemnation, but rather may become for him a pledge of eternal felicity.

274. *What is to be noted immediately before Communion?*

That the priest strikes his breast three times in a spirit of humility, saying: *Domine, non sum dignus*, etc.: "Lord, I am not worthy that Thou should enter under my roof but only say the word and my soul shall be healed."

275. *Why is the bell rung at this moment in many places?*

To alert the faithful who are at a distance from the altar to unite themselves in heart to the priest's Communion, and to draw near to the altar if they are themselves to receive the Holy Eucharist.

276. *Why does the server recite the* Confiteor *before the Communion of the faithful?*

He recites it in the name of all who are about to communicate, because one cannot humble oneself too deeply through the recognition and confession of one's sins before receiving one's God into one's heart; thus all the faithful who are to communicate ought to be kneeling during this recitation of the *Confiteor* by the server.[9]

277. *Why does the celebrant, turned toward the people, repeat three times the* Domine non sum dignus *before giving Communion to the faithful?*

To remind them that it is through His mercy, and not by reason of their own merits, that their Savior is about to give Himself to them; and to rekindle in their hearts the sentiment of humility that ought to fill a Christian in the presence of God, Purity itself, who is about to unite Himself to him.

---

[9] The recitation of the *Confiteor* before Communion was suppressed by John XXIII in 1960.

278. *Why does the priest, after Communion, wash the chalice and his fingers with water and wine?*

In order that not a single drop of the precious Blood of Our Lord may remain in the chalice, nor any particle of the consecrated Host upon the priest's fingers, lest they be inadvertently profaned; for this reason, the priest consumes the water and wine used for these purifications.

279. *What is the sixth part of the Mass?*

It is the THANKSGIVING.

280. *What is meant by the prayers which the priest recites at the Epistle side after Communion?*

They are the prayers of thanksgiving, which, together with the antiphon called the Communion, the *Ite missa est*, the blessing, and the Last Gospel, constitute the sixth part of the Mass.

281. *What is the meaning of* Ite missa est *[Go, the Mass is ended]?*

They are the words by which the priest dismisses the assembly. Formerly, the Mass ended with these words. — One should note that in penitential Masses they are replaced by *Benedicamus Domino*,[10] and in Masses for the dead by *Requiescant in pace*.

282. *How ought one to receive the blessing at the end of Mass?*

One ought to receive it kneeling, making the sign of the cross with profound reverence, and forming the resolution to preserve the fruits of

---

[10] In 1960, the use of the *Benedicamus Domino* was abolished at all Masses except that of Holy Thursday and those followed by a procession.

the Holy Sacrifice just heard, of which this blessing is, as it were, the seal.

283. *What do you know of the origin of the Last Gospel?*

It is said that in former times the faithful, coming in great numbers to have the Gospel *In principio* recited over them, decided to recite it once over the whole congregation, in order to satisfy their devotion.

284. *What do you observe in Masses celebrated before the exposed Blessed Sacrament?*

That the priest genuflects before the tabernacle, rather than making a simple bow, whenever he passes from one side of the altar to the other, or whenever he leaves or returns to the center of the altar; furthermore, he always endeavors, as far as possible, never to turn his back entirely upon the Blessed Sacrament.[11]

285. *What is to be noted in Requiem Masses?*

That: (1) the Psalm *Judica me* and all songs of joy, such as the *Gloria in excelsis*, the *Gloria Patri*, and the *Alleluia*, are omitted; (2) the *Credo*, which belongs properly to more solemn Masses, is not said; (3) there are no blessings, nor is the final blessing of the Mass given; (4) in the *Agnus Dei*, instead of *Miserere nobis*, one says *Dona eis requiem*, without striking the breast; (5) the kiss of peace is not given, and consequently, the first of the three prayers before Communion is omitted.[12]

---

[11] The celebration of Masses before the exposed Blessed Sacrament was prohibited by Paul VI (1963–1978) in 1967.

[12] Additionally, the 1960 rubrics promulgated by John XXIII

§ III.
OF THE HIGH OR SOLEMN MASS

286. *What is meant by a High Mass?*

It is called HIGH MASS when the Mass is celebrated with chant, with more solemn outward ceremonies, and with a greater number of ministers.

287. *What is properly called a Solemn Mass?*

A SOLEMN MASS is properly the High Mass at which the priest is assisted by a deacon and a subdeacon, and not merely by inferior clerics such as altar boys.

288. *What ceremonies precede the High Mass on Sundays?*

They are the blessing of the water and the aspersion.

289. *How is the blessing of the water performed?*

It is done either in the choir[13] or in the sacristy, as desired. The priest, vested in surplice and stole, or in alb and stole of the color of the day, recites or sings several prayers by which he exorcises and blesses the salt and the water, which he then mingles in the Name of the Father, and of the Son, and of the Holy Ghost. Then, having vested in the cope, he performs the aspersion over the faithful.

290. *What is the purpose of this aspersion with holy water?*

It is to purify the faithful from the remains

---

call for the omission of the Last Gospel when Mass is followed by the absolution.

[13] See no. 38.

of their sins, so that they may be made more worthy to assist at the Holy Sacrifice of the Mass, and thus fulfill with fitting devotion the most important obligation of the Sunday.

291. *How ought holy water to be used?*

One ought to use it to make the sign of the cross devoutly upon entering the church; to keep some in the home, and to use it morning and evening, as well as in times of grave danger, whether of body or of soul, such as in a storm, or in time of temptation. He who carries the holy water vessel in the ceremonies ought always to do so with great reverence, and take care not to spill the holy water it contains.

292. *What parts of the Mass are sung?*

All those which the priest recites aloud in Low Masses; that is, everything from the Introit to the Oblation of the bread, except the prayer *Munda cor meum*, which is always said silently before the Gospel. Then follow the Preface, the *Sanctus*, the *Pater noster*, the *Agnus Dei*, the antiphon called the Communion, the prayers after Communion, and the *Ite missa est*; but only prelates impart the final blessing in chant at the end of the Mass.

293. *What does the priest sing at High Mass?*

He sings the Prayers, the Preface, the *Pater noster*, and he intones the *Gloria in excelsis* and the *Credo*; and if there is no deacon, he sings the *Ite missa est*.

294. *By whom is the Epistle chanted?*

It is chanted by the subdeacon.

295. *By whom is the Gospel chanted?*

The Gospel is chanted by the deacon.

296. *What is the purpose of chant and of ceremonies?*

It is to enhance the solemnity of our sacred mysteries, and above all to engage the senses so that the Christian heart may remain more faithfully fixed upon the thought of holy things throughout the Office.

297. *What is the use of incense in the ceremonies of the Church?*

The Church offers incense to God, but she also makes use of it to honor the relics of the saints, the sacred images and paintings, and to manifest reverence for things which she has specially blessed, as well as for her ministers and even for the faithful, her children.

298. *Explain the purpose the Church intends in the various circumstances in which she uses incense.*

The Church offers incense to the Most Holy Trinity and to Our Lord Jesus Christ in the Blessed Sacrament, in order to acknowledge the sovereign dominion of the God of Heaven and earth. But when she burns incense before the relics of the saints, it is to honor the friends of God and those bodies which were temples of the Holy Ghost. In like manner, she commands that the faithful be incensed during solemnities, and their bodies on the day of their burial.

299. *Does incense not also bear a mystical meaning?*

Yes: when offered to God, it represents, according to Holy Scripture (Apocalypse), the prayers of the faithful ascending unto the throne of God; when offered to the ministers of the altar and to the faithful, it reminds them that they must diffuse everywhere the sweet odor of Jesus Christ.

300. *How is incense offered in the Church?*

It is offered kneeling when it is directed to God Himself; in all other cases, it is offered standing.

301. *How is the incensation of the altar performed at solemn Masses?*

The celebrant, after having blessed the incense, turns toward the tabernacle and incenses, standing, the cross above it with three swings; then he incenses with two swings on each side toward the relics or statues placed between the candlesticks (if there be none, he omits this incensation); finally, he incenses the top, the sides, and the front of the altar, on the right and on the left. He then returns the thurible to the deacon, who incenses him with three swings. If the Blessed Sacrament is exposed, the incensation of the tabernacle is performed kneeling. At the Offertory, before the incensation of the altar, the priest incenses the offerings, that is, the host and the chalice. When the incensation of the altar is complete, the clergy and the faithful are incensed.

302. *Why is it that, while the faithful and the lower clergy are incensed as a group with only a few swings, the priests and the ministers of the altar are incensed individually with one or more swings?*

It is to acknowledge in the former the sublimity of the sacerdotal character, and to honor in the latter the privilege granted to them of being admitted to the service of the altar.

303. *How ought the faithful to comport themselves during the incensation of the people?*

All ought to rise.

304. *What is particular to the Elevation at solemn Masses?*

It is that during this august moment, clerics stand near the altar holding torches or great lighted candles, and that the subdeacon or the thurifer incenses the Body and Blood of Our Lord, while the priest elevates them and offers them to the adoration of the faithful.

305. *Why does the subdeacon hold the paten, veiled, from the Offertory until the* Pater noster *at solemn Masses?*

Because in former times the paten, being very large and cumbersome upon the altar, was given to the subdeacon to guard until the moment of Communion. What remains is but a vestige of this ancient custom.[14] The paten is not placed again upon the altar until the priest needs to lay the Sacred Host upon it after having broken it.[15]

---

[14] Others explain the holding of the paten thus: "This practice is...based on the even older custom that in the Masses in the Roman titular churches the acolytes would hold a particle of the host consecrated in the Papal Mass on a reverently covered paten until this so-called *fermentum* was lowered into the chalice in order to express unity with the bishop of Rome" (Michael Fiedrowicz, *The Traditional Mass: History, Form, & Theology of the Classical Roman Rite* [Angelico Press, 2020], 95).

[15] Usually called "the fraction" of the Host.

306. *Why does all the clergy exchange an embrace after the* Agnus Dei *at these Masses?*

It is the kiss of peace which all the faithful once gave one another before going to receive Holy Communion. The clergy alone have retained this ancient usage; but the faithful ought to remember, on seeing this beautiful ceremony, that they must cherish in their hearts, for all their brethren, the charity represented by the kiss of peace among the clergy.

307. *What is the parish Mass?*

This name is given to the solemn Mass sung in parish churches on Sundays and feast days. This Mass is offered with a special intention for the faithful, and includes the sprinkling with holy water [on Sunday], the prayers and announcements of the *prône*, the sermon, the blessing of bread, and the offering of the faithful. In France, the prayer for the State, the *Domine salvam fac*, is sung at this Mass.

308. *What is the* prône?

It is the name given to the gathering of: (1) the public prayers for the Church, the State, and all the faithful, living and dead; (2) the announcements of feasts, fasts, particular ceremonies, and the Masses of the week; (3) the publication of banns of marriage; (4) the reading of the Gospel in the vernacular tongue; and (5) the instruction or sermon delivered by the pastors of the Church to their parishioners on Sundays.[16]

---

[16] This vernacular catechetical practice, including bidding prayers, was widespread throughout western Europe even into

309. *How is the offertory procession made?*[17]

When at Solemn Mass the offering of the clergy and the people takes place, the celebrant descends to the entrance of the sanctuary to receive it. Each person presents himself before the priest, kisses the pax-brede, and places his offering, that is, a coin, according to his means and will.

310. *Whence comes this custom?*

In former times, the faithful brought to the altar the bread, wine, and wax needed for the celebration of the sacred mysteries. Later, the custom arose of no longer offering the things themselves, but the money necessary to purchase them, and this is what endures to this day.

311. *Could you not cite some beautiful vestige of this ancient custom?*

Yes, there are several examples. In many places, during the offices for the dead, three clerics of the church or certain relatives of the deceased present at the offering: one a wax candle, another a loaf of bread, and the third wine in a vessel; the rest of the congregation then presents their offerings in money. — In certain wine-growing regions, as at Argenteuil for instance, at the Mass of thanksgiving following the grape harvest, the head of the vintners offers at the Offertory, in the

---

the twentieth century. It was regulated by diocesan statutes, and not required by the Missal's rubrics.

[17] The offertory procession (*offrande*), although not prescribed in the Roman Missal promulgated by Pius V (1566–1572), was a medieval custom originating in the Gallican rite used in France before the Roman rite became standard. Many dioceses maintained this usage into the twentieth century.

cruet, wine of the new vintage, and this wine is used for the Holy Sacrifice for the consecration of the Precious Blood. A nearly similar custom is found at Chartres and elsewhere: on the sixth day of August, the feast of the Transfiguration of Our Lord, the deacon presses into the chalice a cluster of new grapes which has been offered at the offertory procession.

312. *Can you name another vestige of the offertory procession?*

It is the offering of the blessed bread, which takes place only in France.

313. *What is the origin of the blessed bread?*

Formerly, as the faithful themselves at the offertory procession brought up the bread that was to be consecrated, and there was too much of it, the unconsecrated remainder was distributed to those who did not communicate, to make them share, by a sort of communion, in the graces from which they were deprived. When the offering in kind of the very bread of sacrifice ceased, the faithful took up the custom of presenting bread for the priest's blessing, and this is the origin of the blessed bread, the pious custom of which endures especially in our country.

Chapter II

✠

Of the Divine Office

314. *What is the Divine Office?*

The Divine Office, also called the Canonical Hours, is a collection of prayers arranged in a certain order by the Church to be sung by the faithful united with the priests or recited by the latter in the name of all the faithful who cannot be present each day.

315. *Of what is the Divine Office generally composed?*

It is composed of psalms, antiphons, lessons, hymns, responsories, and orations or prayers drawn up by the Church in a particular form.

316. *With what do the various Hours of the Office begin, and how are they concluded?*

The Hours of the Office all begin with the prayer *Deus in adjutorium*, "O God, come to my assistance," taken from Psalm 69, together with the *Gloria Patri*; and they end with the prayer *Benedicamus Domino*: "Let us bless the Lord." The only exceptions are the three days of Holy Week and the Office of the Dead.

317. *How is the Divine Office divided?*

Into two principal parts, which are called the NIGHT OFFICE and the DAY OFFICE.

318. *What is the name given to the Night Office, and what is its purpose?*

It is called **MATINS**, **NOCTURNS**, or **VIGILS**. Its purpose is to consecrate the rest of the night by prayer, after the example of the prophet David, who "rose in the midst of the night to proclaim the greatness of God."

319. *Are Matins always recited in the middle of the night?*

No, the Church, through indulgence, permits them to be sung or recited in the morning or the evening before. Only religious and certain chapters continue to sing them during the night in our own day.

320. *Of what do Matins consist?*

They consist of a psalm called the **INVITATORY**, a hymn, and one or three **NOCTURNS**, that is, prayers of the night. The single nocturn comprises twelve psalms and three lessons. When there are three nocturns, as on feasts and offices of higher rank, each consists of three psalms, three lessons, and as many responsories. The first nocturn on Sunday is preceded by twelve psalms before the first set of lessons.[1]

321. *Why is the psalm that begins Matins called the Invitatory?*

Because it is an invitation to praise the Lord. The antiphon repeated after several verses almost always ends with the words: *Venite, adoremus,*

---

[1] According to the Breviary reforms of Pius X (1903–1914), promulgated by the bull *Divino afflatu* in 1911, Matins on Sundays and major feasts has three nocturns, each always having three psalms, lessons, and responsories. On ferias and minor feasts, a single nocturn of nine psalms is said, followed by three lessons and responsories.

"Come, let us adore [the Lord]." — This psalm is also sung in the Office of the Dead, but only at solemn Vigils.

322. *What are hymns?*

They are joyful songs composed in honor of God, the Blessed Virgin, and the Saints. They are not used in the mournful offices of Holy Week or the Office of the Dead.

323. *What are the psalms?*

They are the canticles composed by the prophet David, in which he sings of the greatness and goodness of God.[2] The psalms form the greater part of the Divine Office.

324. *What are antiphons?*

They are prayers or maxims, most often drawn from the psalms, sung before and after the psalms, or only after them when the office is not of double rank.[3]

325. *What are responsories?*

Responsories are much like antiphons. They are called responsories because, after a verse is sung by a few voices, the whole choir responds

---

[2] It should be noted that the Book of Psalms attributes a number of psalms to authors other than King David, including his son Solomon.

[3] Prior to the reforms of Pius XII and John XXIII, liturgical days were ranked as followed (lowest to highest): Feria; Simple; Semidouble; Lesser Double; Greater/Major Double; Double of the Second Class; Double of the First Class. In the major hours, only on Doubles would the antiphon be said in full before and after the Psalm. On lower-ranking feasts, in all hours, the incipit, or beginning, of the antiphon would be said before the psalm and the entire antiphon afterwards. Minor Hours all observed the incipit-then-full scheme.

by repeating part of the antiphon. — **BRIEF RESPONSORIES** are very short responses, such as *In manus tuas* at Compline. There is a brief responsory at each of the Little Hours.

326. *What are the lessons?*

They are passages from Scripture or from the writings of the holy Doctors, which the Church commands to be read during the night offices. They are a form of reading: for this reason, their chant is very simple.

327. *What is the* Te Deum*?*

It is a canticle in honor of the Most Holy Trinity, believed to have been composed by Saint Ambrose and Saint Augustine. It always concludes the Night Office on feast days. It is also sung on certain occasions to give thanks to God for some happy event for the Church, the State, or the parish; but then only by order or with the permission of the diocesan bishop.

328. *What are Lauds?*

Lauds, or **MORNING PRAISES**, are the prayers of the Office that were once sung, and are still sung by religious, at the break of dawn. They ordinarily follow Matins.

329. *How is the Day Office divided?*

It comprises several Hours of prayer called Prime, Terce, Sext, None, Vespers, and Compline.

330. *What is Prime?*

It is the first of the so-called **LITTLE HOURS**, in contrast with Matins, Lauds, and Vespers, which are longer and more solemn. It is called Prime because it is sung at six o'clock in the morning, which the ancients called the first hour of the day.

331. *What was the Church's intention in instituting this prayer of the first hour?*

The Church's intention was to consecrate the Christian's day to God and to offer Him all its actions, as may be clearly seen by the reading of the prayers in this office.

332. *What are Terce, Sext, and None?*

They are the prayers sung at nine o'clock in the morning, formerly called the third hour of the day; at noon, which was the sixth hour; and at three o'clock, which was the ninth.

333. *Of what do these three Little Hours consist?*

After the *Deus in adjutorium*, one sings a hymn of three stanzas. — Then three sections of Psalm 118,[4] each followed by the *Gloria Patri*, an antiphon, a short chapter, a brief responsory, and the collect of the Mass of the day.

334. *What mysteries does the Church honor in these various hours?*

At Terce, the Church seeks to honor the descent of the Holy Ghost upon the Apostles; at Sext, the crucifixion of Our Lord; at None, His death upon the Cross for the salvation of mankind: three mysteries that took place at those very hours.

---

[4] Prior to the reform of the Breviary by Pius X, Psalm 118 was recited daily, divided over the Hours of Prime, Terce, Sext, and None. As a result of this reform, Psalm 118 is prayed in these Hours only on Sundays and major feasts.

335. *What are Vespers?*

Vespers are the portion of the Office that is sung in the evening (in Latin: *Horæ Vespertinæ*, "the evening hours").

336. *Of what do Vespers consist?*

Vespers consist of five psalms with their respective antiphons, a hymn, and the canticle of the Most Blessed Virgin with its antiphon. They conclude with a collect and the chant of the *Benedicamus*.

337. *What is Compline?*

Compline, in Latin *Completorium*, is the Hour which completes or ends the Christian day. It is that portion of the Office which was sung, and is still sung by religious, at the close of day. It is truly the EVENING PRAYER, and the most beautiful of all.

338. *How is this Hour of the Office arranged?*

After a brief lesson sung by the reader and the Lord's Prayer, the officiant and the choir alternate in reciting the *Confiteor* in confession of sins. Then are sung four psalms,[5] the antiphon *Miserere*, the hymn *Te lucis ante terminum*, which is properly a prayer for a good and holy night; a short chapter, the brief responsory *In manus*, the canticle of Saint Simeon, *Nunc dimittis*, and a collect; the officiant then gives the blessing,

---

[5] Prior to the reform of the Breviary by Pius X, Compline would consist of the same four Psalms every day: 4, 30:2-6, 90, and 133. Following this reform, the number of Psalms at Compline were reduce to three and vary day-by-day. However, on Sundays and major Feasts, Psalms 4, 90, and 133 are prayed.

and finally one sings an antiphon to the Blessed Virgin. After this antiphon, the Office of the day ends with the *Pater noster, Ave Maria*, and *Credo*, which each one recites in a low voice.[6]

339. *Which are the most solemn Hours of the Office?*

They are Matins, Lauds, and Vespers, at which the officiant and his ministers vest in copes on solemn feasts. — At Lauds and Vespers, during the canticle that concludes them, the altar is incensed with the same ceremonial as at the solemn Mass.

340. *Why does the rubric prescribe making the sign of the cross when the cantors begin the* Benedictus *at Lauds, the* Magnificat *at Vespers, and the* Nunc dimittis *at Compline?*

Because these three canticles are taken from the holy Gospel.

341. *What general observations may be made about the Office of the Dead?*

(1) The Office of the Dead has neither Little Hours nor Compline; it consists only of First Vespers, Matins, and Lauds;[7] (2) the *Gloria Patri* is not sung, but in its stead is said: *Requiem æternam dona eis Domine*, etc.: "Lord, grant them eternal rest…"; (3) hymns are never sung therein, nor the *Te Deum*.

---

[6] These three silent prayers were suppressed in 1960.

[7] These are Hours which could be prayed daily and even incorporated into the publicly celebrated Hours, immediately following the day's Lauds and Vespers. They could also be part of the funeral rites. A full Office of the Dead for the Commemoration of All Souls, including the Little Hours and Compline, was introduced by Pius X in 1911.

342. *With what dispositions ought one to assist at the Office of the Dead?*

One must pray fervently for the departed soul and for all the faithful departed, reflect that death shall likewise one day come for us, and implore from God the grace to die in justice and to be reconciled with the sovereign Judge.

343. *What is the best manner of assisting at the Offices of the Church?*

It is to follow them as closely as possible, and to sing with the choir if one knows how and has the strength; but care must be taken never to sing when the ministers of the choir are chanting alone, such as at the intonations, and above all, when it is the officiant who is chanting.

344. *What ought one to observe in standing, sitting, or kneeling during the Office?*

The best way of performing these actions fittingly is to follow the movements of the choir.

CHAPTER III

✠

Of Certain Particular Ceremonies

§ I.
OF PROCESSIONS

345. *What are processions?*

Processions are ceremonies in which one advances in orderly manner while reciting prayers.

346. *What is the purpose of processions?*

It varies according to the occasion: some are instituted to celebrate joyful mysteries; others are undertaken to pray to the Blessed Virgin and the Saints, as, for example, during a solemn pilgrimage; but most are exercises of penance. The third part of this catechism speaks of the particular purpose of each of the processions held throughout the year.

347. *Why is the cross carried at the head of processions?*

To teach us that we can reach Heaven only by following Jesus crucified; and for this reason the crucifix is turned forward, to represent more perfectly the Savior of the world going before us and tracing the path of salvation.

348. *What does the deacon do at the moment the procession sets out from the church?*

He turns toward the faithful and sings: *Procedamus in pace*: "Let us go forth in peace"; and the people respond: *In nomine Christi, Amen*: "In the name of Jesus Christ, Amen." This is to teach us that we can have no peace in this world unless our steps and our actions conform to the examples and the will of Our Lord.

§ II.
OF THE BENEDICTION OF THE MOST BLESSED SACRAMENT

349. *What is Benediction?*

It is a ceremony that ordinarily takes place in the evening, after the Office, whose principal act is the blessing given to the faithful with the Blessed Sacrament, whether enclosed in the ciborium or exposed visibly in the monstrance.

350. *Is one of these two forms of Benediction better than the other?*

It would be a grave error to think so, for in either case, it is Jesus Christ Himself, truly present in the Eucharist, who deigns to bless us.

351. *Of what does Benediction consist?*

When solemnly celebrated, it consists at the very least of the *Tantum ergo*, with its versicle and the Collect of the Blessed Sacrament. In various dioceses, approved customs permit the *Tantum ergo* to be preceded by several hymns in honor of the Blessed Virgin or the Saints, and for the Sovereign Pontiff.

352. *How ought one to assist at Benediction?*

In sentiments of profound reverence for the Real Presence of Our Lord, and with deep gratitude for the blessing which He Himself is pleased to bestow upon us through the hands of His minister.

§ III.
OF THE CEREMONIES USED IN THE ADMINISTRATION OF THE SACRAMENTS

353. *What are the most striking ceremonies in the administration of the sacrament of baptism?*

They are the EXORCISMS, or the prayers by which the devil is cast out of the child's body; the salt placed in the mouth, with represents wisdom; the infusion of water, or the baptism properly so called, by which the soul is cleansed from the stain of original sin; the anointings, by which the priest consecrates this new temple of the Holy Ghost; the Chrisom, a small white linen cloth or cap placed upon the child's head after the anointing with holy chrism, and which is the symbol of the robe of innocence that the Christian must preserve without stain until the judgment of God;[1] finally, the lighted candle, which represents the faith and charity that ought to remain ever-burning and luminous in our hands, that we may go forth to meet Jesus Christ when He comes to judge us.

---

[1] Where a white garment is used, it is placed first on the newly baptized baby's head before being worn. Adults can be given both the chrisom and a white garment to wear.

354. *What sentiments ought a Christian to foster in his heart when assisting at a baptism?*

He ought to renew the promises of his own baptism, to thank God for admitting another soul into the number of His children, and to beg for the newly baptized the grace of perseverance in doing good and fidelity to his baptismal promises.

355. *With what sentiments ought a Christian child to assist the priest who is giving Holy Communion?*

He ought to stir within himself the desire to receive the Holy Eucharist, and to ask God for the grace to make a good First Communion.

356. *What should one note in the administration of extreme unction?*

One ought to note the entrance of the priest into the house, to which he first wishes the peace of the Lord; the sprinkling of holy water, by which he drives away the spirit of evil; and lastly, the anointings made upon the sick person's members to purify him from the remnants of sin. These anointings are as it were a new consecration of this temple of the Holy Ghost, too often defiled by sin.

357. *How ought one to accompany the priest to the house of the sick?*

With modest and composed deportment, expressing compassion for the sorrow of the afflicted family; mindful that, sooner or later, according to the will of the Lord, one shall oneself reach that same extremity; and asking God not to die without receiving the last sacraments.

358. *What ought one to do when present at the touching ceremony of the ordination of priests and other ministers of the altar?*

A good Christian ought to pray for the clerics whom he sees receiving Holy Orders, that they may all become worthy ministers of the holy Church; to follow attentively the ordination rites, which are most edifying; and finally, to receive with reverence and devotion the blessing given by the bishop at the conclusion of the ceremony.

359. *What ought one to avoid when attending a marriage?*

One ought to avoid distractions, and pray for the spouses, that God may bless their union and render it happy both on earth and in Heaven.

§ IV.
OF CHRISTIAN BURIAL

360. *What is the final mark of tenderness that our holy Mother the Church bestows upon her children?*

It is the last prayers offered over their mortal remains, and the solemn ceremonies of Christian burial.

361. *How are the funeral rites conducted?*

The clergy proceed to the house of the deceased. Upon arriving near the coffin, the *De profundis* is recited. The body is then taken and carried to the church while the *Miserere* is sung. Upon arrival at the church, the sublime responsory *Subvenite* is sung, followed by the Mass of the Dead or some part of the Office of the Dead, depending on the circumstances. At the foot of the coffin prayers known as the ABSOLUTION are recited, during which the body is sprinkled and incensed; it is then brought to the cemetery while the antiphon *In Paradisum* is sung: "May the angels lead you into Paradise." At the graveside, the *Benedictus* is chanted, with the antiphon *Ego sum resurrectio*: "I am the Resurrection," etc. The body is again sprinkled and incensed during the *Pater noster*. Finally, when the coffin is lowered into the grave, the priest casts holy water upon it, chants once more *Requiescat in pace*: "May he rest in peace," and the clergy withdraw.

362. *What is the general spirit of the Church's prayers during interments or funeral offices?*

The Church always places upon the lips of those present, in the name of the departed, words of repentance, supplications for mercy, and thoughts of hope. At times she also addresses the departed directly, with wishes full of tenderness and confidence in the goodness of God. For example, in the verse of the responsory *Subvenite: Suscipiat te Christus*, etc.: "May Our Lord Jesus Christ, who called thee, receive thee, and may the Angels lead thee into the bosom of Abraham." Likewise, in the antiphon *In paradisum*: "May the Angels lead thee into Paradise, may the martyrs receive thee at thy coming, and bring thee into the holy city Jerusalem; may thou have eternal rest near Lazarus, who once was poor."

363. *Why are candles carried at funerals, and placed near the departed?*

Several reasons may be given: (1) The candles bear witness to the fervor of the prayers offered for the departed by those who carry them; (2) Placed around the body, they signify the ardor of his faith during life, and the hope he held in a future life, wherein he is to enjoy the light of God; (3) They do honor even unto the last remains of a child of the Church, and of a body marked more than once with holy oil.

364. *Why is holy water used at funerals?*

That a full grace of pardon for the sins of the departed may be obtained from God.

365. *Why is the body of the departed incensed?*

That one last honor may be rendered unto that body which was the temple of the Holy Ghost and is destined to rise again one day.

366. *How is the body of the faithful placed in the church?*

It is placed with the face turned towards the altar. Priests, on the contrary, are placed with the face turned towards the people, as though they would still instruct them, even as they did in life.

367. *What is the manner of burying bishops, priests, and clerics?*

They are placed in their coffin vested in the ornaments of their order, which are of violet color. Bishops and priests are clad as though to offer the Holy Sacrifice of the Mass. Simple clerics or those in minor orders are vested in cassock and surplice; religious and nuns in the habit of their order.

368. *What is particular to the funerals of little children?*

(1) When they are buried, a crown of fragrant flowers is placed upon their head as a sign of their innocence; (2) The priest wears white ornaments, and only songs of joy are sung; (3) At their funeral procession, a cross without a staff is carried to signify that their days have been shortened and that their pilgrimage on earth was brief.

369. *Why does the Church, who uses songs of sorrow at the funerals of older persons, sing songs of joy at the burial of little children who have died with baptism?*

Because these children, having had no use of reason, could not offend God, and their salvation is assured; and the Church can only rejoice to see them delivered from the sufferings of this life and admitted to the happiness of Heaven.

370. *What is meant by a service?*

This name is given to the offices celebrated for one or more departed souls some time after their death or upon the anniversary of their passing.

✠

THE FEASTS OF THE CHURCH, OR THE LITURGICAL YEAR

CHAPTER I

✠

Classification and Degrees of the Feasts of the Roman Church

371. *How are the Church's solemnities divided?*

They are divided into the Proper of Time and the Proper of Saints, according as the office is celebrated in keeping with the season in which one finds oneself, or according to the feasts which the Church has instituted in honor of the mysteries of the Blessed Virgin and of the Saints.

372. *How is the Proper of Time divided?*

It is divided into Sundays and Ferias, and comprises five great seasons: the season of ADVENT, the season of CHRISTMAS and EPIPHANY, the season of SEPTUAGESIMA and LENT, the season of EASTER, and the SUNDAYS AFTER PENTECOST.

373. *What is meant by Sundays and Ferias?*

Sunday is the day consecrated unto the Lord, when one must assist at the offices and abstain from labor. The FERIAS, or weekdays, are those upon which no feast hinders the pursuit of ordinary occupations. In the language of the Church, one says that the office of the feria or of the Sunday is made when no saint's feast is celebrated on that day; then the office is taken from the Proper of Time.

374. *What do you mean by privileged Sundays and Ferias?*

Privileged Sundays are those which do not admit any feast. Privileged Ferias do not admit simple feasts, and one must always make commemoration of such ferias when their proper Office is not celebrated. There are also major ferias, which admit no feast whatsoever, such as the Octave of the Epiphany, the fortnight of Easter,[1] and the Octave of Pentecost.

375. *What are the ranks of Feasts?*

The highest rank is the DOUBLE OF THE FIRST CLASS: these are the greatest solemnities, such as Christmas, Easter, Pentecost, etc. Next come the DOUBLE OF THE SECOND CLASS, the GREATER DOUBLE, the LESSER DOUBLE, and the SEMI-DOUBLE, which yields to the Sunday, being of the same rank but less worthy; lastly comes the SIMPLE, which is the least solemn of all feasts and is only commemorated on privileged ferias.[2]

376. *What is an octave?*

An octave of a feast is the eight-day period during which the Office or the commemoration of that feast is made, counting from the day of the solemnity itself.

377. *What is a privileged octave?*

It is one which does not admit any other Office than that of the feast whose octave is being

---

[1] That is, Holy Week and the Octave of Easter.
[2] In 1960, John XXIII dramatically simplified the rankings, dividing liturgical days into those of the first, second, third, and fourth class.

celebrated. Such are the octaves of the Epiphany, of Easter, and of Pentecost.[3]

378. *What does it mean to make a commemoration of a Feast, a Saint, or a Feria?*

It consists in reciting at Matins one lesson from those Offices, and recalling them: (1) at Lauds and FIRST VESPERS,[4] by an antiphon, a versicle, and a collect; (2) at Mass, by the three prayers: the COLLECT, the SECRET, and the POSTCOMMUNION.

---

[3] In 1955, Pius XII suppressed all Octaves save those of Christmas, Easter, and Pentecost.

[4] In keeping with ancient Jewish usage according to which a day began the evening before (thus, Sabbath began Friday evening and continued until Saturday evening), Sundays and feastdays liturgically began the evening before with First Vespers. Under the changes imposed by Pius XII and John XXIII, feasts generally liturgically begin with Matins, while First Vespers is limited to Sundays and major feasts.

CHAPTER II

✠

The Proper of Time

§ I.
OF ADVENT

379. *When does the Christian year begin?*
It begins on the First Sunday of Advent.

380. *What is Advent?*
The name Advent is given to the four weeks which precede the feast of Christmas.

381. *What does the word Advent mean?*
It means coming or arrival.

382. *Whose coming is awaited during Advent?*
That of the Child Jesus, our Savior.

383. *What do the four Sundays of Advent represent?*
They represent the four thousand years which preceded the coming of Jesus Christ upon earth.

384. *What do you remark as particular in the Church's ceremonies during the season of Advent?*
Two things: the violet ornaments and the chanting of the *Rorate*.

385. *Why does the Church use violet ornaments?*
Because in her mind violet signifies penance, as has been explained in speaking of the color of the ornaments (see nos. 171 and 172).

386. *Why does the Church use penitential vestments?*

Because Advent was formerly a season of penance, though less rigorous than Lent; and the Church, while dispensing from fasting, has wished nonetheless to preserve the signs of mourning in her Offices, in order to move us to prepare ourselves by mortification to worthily receive the Child Jesus on Christmas.

387. *Why is the* Gloria in excelsis *not sung at the Masses of the Advent season?*

It is always in the same spirit of penance that the Church abstains from this song of joy.

388. *But why is the Alleluia sung?*

The Church sings it, and even more frequently than on ordinary Sundays, because, while she prepares for the coming of Jesus Christ by penance and prayer, she is filled with joy in the hope of soon beholding this God-Child.

389. *What do you think of the* Rorate *that is sung in our churches?*

It is a beautiful prayer, whose very melody inspires devotion. This prayer, however, is not a universal song of the Church. It is granted to certain dioceses of France by privilege. One must enter deeply into the sentiments of pious expectation expressed by the prophet, and sing with faith the words *Rorate cœli*, etc.: "Drop down dew, ye heavens, from above, and let the clouds rain down the Just."[1]

---

[1] This hymn, composed in the early seventeenth century by members of the French Oratory, was extremely popular in France, being sung daily throughout Advent at evening services.

390. *What is special about the Third Sunday of Advent?*

At the solemn Mass, the signs of joy that had been laid aside are resumed: the altar is adorned with flowers, all the bells are rung, the organ is played, and the deacon and subdeacon wear dalmatics instead of being vested only in albs,[2] as on the other Sundays of Advent.

391. *Why is this so?*

Because of the words of the Introit: *Gaudete*, "Rejoice." The Church invites us to hope, for the coming of Jesus Christ, our Redeemer, is near.

392. *Do you know of anything particular in the last days of Advent?*

There are what are called the *O* Antiphons of Christmas.

393. *What are the* O *Antiphons of Christmas?*

This is the common name given to seven antiphons of the Office in the last days of Advent,[3] each of which begins with the invocation *O*.

394. *What do these antiphons represent?*

They represent the longing desires of the patriarchs of the Old Law, who yearned for the coming of the Savior.

395. *How are these antiphons sung?*

---

[2] More properly, the Tridentine Missal specified that deacons and subdeacons during penitential seasons wear chasubles folded in the front instead of their usual dalmatic and tunic. Where folded chasubles were unavailable, as was the case in smaller parishes, the deacons and subdeacons were to wear only albs.

[3] That is, December 17 to 23 inclusively.

They are sung during the seven days preceding Christmas, once before the *Magnificat* and once after.

396. *Do you know of any pious custom concerning these antiphons?*

Yes, in certain countries, Vespers are still sung in the evening during these seven days. They are called the "O Vespers of Christmas." Elsewhere, Vespers are only sung from the hymn *Creator alme siderum* onwards, or even merely the *Magnificat* with the O antiphon, which is then repeated, and afterward the Benediction of the Blessed Sacrament is given: the faithful commonly refer to this devotion as "the O Salutations of Christmas." Devout souls ought to take delight in attending this pious exercise, in order to prepare themselves more fittingly for the feast of Christmas.

§ II.
OF THE VIGIL OF CHRISTMAS
AND VIGILS IN GENERAL

397. *What does the word* vigil *mean?*
The word "vigil" means "watch."[4]

398. *What does this word* watch *recall?*
It recalls the ancient practice of the faithful who spent the night before great feasts in prayer.

---

[4] It seems that the word "vigil" originally designated the overnight Office. There was a shift in names, so that the penitential day of preparation before a major feast came to be called "the vigil" while the overnight office was called "Matins." A "Vigil Mass" is, therefore, the Mass of a Vigil Day, proper to it — *not* the Mass of a feast or Sunday said the evening before to allow fulfillment of an obligation (such a Mass is properly called an "anticipated Mass").

399. *Is this no longer done?*

No, especially since the last century, though one cannot say that these watches have entirely disappeared, even in France.

400. *What remains of this custom?*

What remains is, on the eve of the greatest feasts, fasting for all the faithful, the use of violet vestments, and penitential prayers within a longer Office.

401. *Is the Office of the Vigils then a penitential Office?*

Yes, for the purpose of the Vigils is to prepare for the morrow's solemnity, which is best accomplished by penance.

402. *Do you know of any other remnants of the ancient Vigils?*

Yes, the Matins of the Dead, which have retained the name "Vigils" to signify that they ought to be recited during the night beside the remains of the departed, as is still practiced in religious communities and in countries where piety prevails.

403. *What is the feast in which we find the most traces of the ancient watches or Vigils?*

It is the holy night of Christmas, a great part of which we still spend in church, singing God's praises at the Offices of Matins and Lauds, and during which the Midnight Mass is solemnly celebrated.

§ III.
FROM THE FEAST AND SEASON OF CHRISTMAS

404. *On what day is the feast of Christmas celebrated?*
On the twenty-fifth of December.

405. *What does the word* Noël *mean?*
Noël means "nativity" or "birth."

406. *Whose birth is celebrated?*
The birth of Our Lord Jesus Christ, the Son of God made man.

407. *What passage of the Christmas Office best recalls this mystery?*
The words from the Gospel of Saint John: "And the Word was made flesh, and dwelt among us," in Latin: *Et Verbum caro factum est*, etc.

408. *What do you find most noteworthy in the feast of Christmas?*
That every priest celebrates, or at least may celebrate, three Masses on that day.[5]

409. *What are these three Masses?*
The Midnight Mass, the Mass at Dawn, and the Mass of the Day. [Each of these Masses has distinct antiphons, orations, and readings.]

410. *What does the Church desire to teach us through the Midnight Mass?*

---

[5] The universal practice of celebrating three Masses also on All Souls Day, November 2, dates from the pontificate of Benedict XV (1914–1922) and was instituted during World War I.

She desires that we honor the temporal birth of Jesus Christ in the stable of Bethlehem, and the adoration of the angels at the very moment of the Savior's nativity.

411. *And through the Mass at Dawn?*

The Church would have us honor the spiritual birth of Jesus Christ in our hearts by faith, and the adoration of the shepherds.

412. *And, finally, through the Mass of the Day?*

At this third Mass the Church would have us honor the eternal birth of Jesus Christ in the bosom of His Father.

413. *When does the Office of Christmas begin?*

On the eve, at First Vespers, as with all the great feasts.

414. *Are these Vespers sung solemnly?*

The First Vespers of the great feasts are sung in all cathedrals and in some larger churches; but in other parishes, they are sung only when the feast falls on a Monday, and then they are celebrated with great solemnity.[6]

415. *When are the Matins of Christmas sung?*

Before the Midnight Mass, that is, around ten o'clock in the evening.

416. *And the Lauds?*

---

[6] Because parishes frequently celebrated solemn Vespers on Sundays, it follows that if Christmas fell on a Monday, the Vespers usually celebrated on Sunday evening would be First Vespers of Christmas.

Immediately after the Midnight Mass, of which they are a kind of thanksgiving.

417. *What do these prayers on Christmas night represent?*

They recall the night watches of the shepherds as they made their way to the Infant Jesus, and tended their flocks.

418. *Why is a Mass celebrated at midnight?*

Because, according to Christian tradition, Our Lord was born at midnight.

419. *At what time is the Mass at dawn said?*

In the early morning.

420. *What Gospel is read at the Mass of the day, that is, the third Mass?*

The beginning of the Gospel according to Saint John is read, where we find the words: "And the Word was made flesh," etc.

421. *Why do we kneel at these words?*

It is to adore the Son of God made man for our salvation, and to express to God our gratitude for so great a mercy.

422. *Is there not another moment when we also kneel?*

Yes, at the Creed, at the words: *Et incarnatus est ... homo factus est*, and for the same reason as mentioned in number 250.[7]

---

[7] As per rubrics, on Christmas and on the Feast of the Annunciation the priest and ministers *must* kneel during the sung *Incarnatus est* of the *Credo* in addition to their genuflection during the read recitation. On other days, however, they

423. *What particular gesture accompanies the hymn at Vespers on Christmas Day?*

It is that while intoning it, the priest extends his hands, raises them, and joins them again, no doubt because of the invocation with which it begins: "Jesus, Redeemer of all," *Jesu, Redemptor omnium.*

424. *What is the proper hymn of the Christmas season?*

It is the *Adeste fideles* ("O Come, All Ye Faithful").

425. *What is the purpose of this hymn?*

It is to invite the faithful to adore the Infant Jesus in His crib.

426. *What are the feasts of the week of Christmas?*

They are: (1) the feast of Saint Stephen, the first martyr, one of the first seven deacons of the Church; it is the feast of deacons; (2) the feast of Saint John, Apostle and Evangelist; it is the feast of priests; (3) lastly, the feast of the Holy Innocents, which has for many centuries been the feast of subdeacons and of altar boys.

427. *What feast does the Church celebrate on the octave day of Christmas?*

It is the Circumcision of Our Lord, who on this day received the name of Jesus, which means "Savior."

428. *What sentiments ought to animate a Christian on this feast?*

With reverence and love for the name of Jesus.

---

may be seated after reciting it and would simply bow their heads at this time.

429. *How can a Christian honor the Name of Jesus?*

By never pronouncing it except with reverence, and by bowing the head slightly when this sacred Name is sung.

430. *With what favor does the Church reward this pious practice?*

She grants indulgences to those who observe it, and likewise to those who do the same at the *Gloria Patri*.

431. *Is there not some particular ceremony on the day of the Circumcision?*

Yes, since it is the first day of the year, it is customary in certain countries to chant the *Veni Creator* to implore the light of the Holy Ghost for the worthy beginning of the new year; and likewise in many dioceses, it is customary on December 31 to chant the *Te Deum*, in thanksgiving for the graces God has bestowed upon us during the year now ending.

§ IV.

FROM EPIPHANY TO SEPTUAGESIMA

432. *What feast does the Church celebrate after the Circumcision?*

The feast of the Epiphany of Our Lord, on the sixth of January.

433. *What does the word* epiphany *mean?*

Epiphany means "manifestation"; it is the feast of the manifestation of Our Lord.

434. *What is the Church's intention in this feast?*

It is to honor the three miracles of the Savior's manifestations: His manifestation to the Magi, who came to adore Him, guided by a mysterious star; His manifestation at His baptism, when a voice proclaimed Him the Son of God; and His manifestation at the wedding feast of Cana, where He performed His first miracle. In the spirit of the Church, we ought to celebrate on this day our vocation to the Christian faith in the persons of the Magi, to whom Jesus Christ revealed His divinity, and to give thanks for so great a grace.

435. *Does the Epiphany have a Vigil?*

Yes, because it is a very great feast.[8]

436. *What particular custom is observed on the Epiphany?*

At the solemn Mass, in certain churches, after the Gospel, the deacon announces the days upon which Easter and the movable feasts will fall in the year.

437. *What is particular about the octave of the Epiphany?*

It is that this octave is privileged (see no. 377).[9]

438. *How many Sundays are there after the Epiphany?*

There are from two to six, depending on the date of Easter.

---

[8] This Vigil was suppressed by Pius XII in 1955.
[9] This octave was suppressed by Pius XII in 1955.

439. *What is the solemnity that falls between the Epiphany and Lent?*

It is the Purification of the Blessed Virgin.

440. *What is particular to this feast?*

It is the blessing of candles, which has given the feast the name CANDLEMAS.

441. *Why did the Church institute this feast?*

To remind us that Jesus Christ is the true Light of the world, and that we ought to follow Him with joy, like the holy old man Simeon, whose words are sung during the distribution of the candles, words that form the antiphon *Lumen ad revelationem gentium*, which is repeated on this occasion after each verse of the *Nunc dimittis*.

442. *Of what material must these candles be made?*

Of genuine wax (see no. 75).

443. *May they be used for profane purposes, for instance, to give light in one's house?*

No, that would show little respect for candles blessed by the prayers of the Church.

444. *For what purposes may the candles be used?*

They may be lit in the home during a storm, during prayer, before a holy image or an altar, beside the bed of a dying person or of the departed.

445. *What is done with the candles during the Mass of Candlemas?*

They are held lit in the hand during the procession, at the Gospel, and from the Elevation until after Communion.

§ V.
FROM SEPTUAGESIMA TO LENT

446. *What are the names of the three Sundays preceding Lent?*

They are called the Sundays of Septuagesima, Sexagesima, and Quinquagesima.

447. *What do these words mean?*

They mean that from these Sundays there remain seventy, sixty, and fifty days respectively until the great feast of Easter.

448. *What is particular to the Office of these Sundays?*

From the first of them, Septuagesima, the Church begins to instill in us the spirit of penance.

449. *By what signs do you recognize this intention of the Church?*

It is that she clothes herself in violet ornaments, ceases to sing the *Gloria in excelsis*, and above all the Alleluia, which is sung twice after the *Benedicamus* at Vespers on the Saturday before Septuagesima, and is no longer sung until the Gradual of the Mass on Holy Saturday.

450. *What is particular to Quinquagesima Sunday and the Monday and Tuesday which follow it?*

It is the devotion of the Forty Hours, which is nevertheless not a general or obligatory observance.

451. *Of what does this devotion consist?*

It consists of exposing the Blessed Sacrament during these three days for the whole day, or at least during the parish Masses and the Benediction sung in the evening on each of those same days.

452. *What is sung during these devotions?*

One commonly sings, along with the usual prayers of Benediction of the Blessed Sacrament, the psalm *Miserere* or the Tract *Domine non secundum*, which are songs of penitence.

453. *What is the purpose of the Forty Hours' devotion?*

It is to ask pardon of God for all the sinful excesses of the carnival, and for all the grievous offences committed by so many Christians during those days of worldly festivity.

454. *How ought a Christian child to conduct himself during these three days?*

He ought, before all else, to abstain from wearing a costume and even from mingling with bands of masqueraders; to assist devoutly at the exposition and Benediction of the Blessed Sacrament; and finally, to pray well and to adore God with all his heart, in reparation for the outrages committed against Him.

§ VI.
FROM ASH WEDNESDAY
AND LENT TO HOLY WEEK

455. *What is Lent?*

Lent is a fast and a season of penance lasting forty days, instituted by the Church to prepare the faithful for the feast of Easter.

456. *When does Lent begin?*
It begins on the Wednesday following Quin-quagesima Sunday.

457. *What is the name given to this first day of Lent?*
It is called ASH WEDNESDAY.

458. *Why is it so called?*
Because on that day ashes are blessed and imposed in the form of a cross upon the heads of the faithful.

459. *Can you tell us something of the manner in which the ashes are blessed?*
A plate is placed upon the altar at the Epistle side, containing ashes made from the blessed branches of the previous year; the celebrant, vested in a violet cope, approaches the altar and recites over these ashes several prayers which express the mind of the Church; then he sprinkles them with holy water and incenses them thrice.

460. *How does the celebrant receive the ashes?*
The first in the choir gives them to the celebrant, who receives them standing, his face turned toward the people. But if the celebrant is the only priest, he kneels before the altar, sets down the plate containing the ashes, and imposes them upon his own tonsure in silence.

461. *How is the imposition of ashes then performed?*
The celebrant imposes them in the form of a cross: upon the tonsure for the ecclesiastics, upon the forehead for the other ministers of the choir and all the faithful, saying in Latin these words:

Memento homo quia pulvis es et in pulverem reverteris: "Remember, man, that thou art dust, and to dust thou shalt return."

462. *What is the Church's purpose in this ceremony?*

It is to recall to us the thought of death and the necessity of doing penance.

463. *How do the ashes remind us of penance?*

Because in former times, when the Church subjected someone to public penance, the bishop would place ashes upon his head and forbid him entry into the church for a time more or less long. Although she no longer maintains such severity in her outward acts of penance, the Church has preserved the memory of that practice in the ceremonies of this day.

464. *With what dispositions ought we to receive the ashes?*

With the thought that one day we must die, and that we must prepare for it by weeping over our sins; we ought also to resolve to pass Lent in a holy manner.

465. *What is the name of the first Sunday of Lent?*

It is called the Sunday of Quadragesima, that is, the fortieth day before Easter.

466. *What are the names of the three following Sundays?*

They are called *Reminiscere, Oculi*, and *Lætare*.

467. *What do these names signify?*

They are the opening words of the Introit of the

Mass for each of those Sundays. Of old, the faithful referred to all the Sundays of the year in this way.

468. *What is particular to Lætare Sunday?*

On that day, the Church invites us to joy by her outward ceremonies, as she already did on the third Sunday of Advent (see no. 390).

469. *Why this unwonted solemnity in a season of penance?*

The first reason for this joy of the Church is that, in former times, this was the day of the scrutiny of the catechumens who were to receive baptism on Holy Saturday. The Church also seeks thereby to rekindle our confidence in the midst of Lenten penance, by showing us that the sacred forty days are already advancing, and that God is soon to pardon our sins. This is the meaning of the words she gives us in the Introit: "Rejoice, all you who have been in sorrow."

470. *What is the particular hymn of Lent in most of our churches?*

It is the chant *Attende, Domine*.

471. *What sentiments does this chant express?*

Sentiments of penance and contrition.

472. *Can you cite an example?*

One may take, for example, the words repeated by the choir at the end of each verse: *Attende, Domine et miserere, quia peccavimus tibi*: "Look upon Thy people, O Lord, and have mercy on us, for we have sinned against Thee."

473. *Why are Vespers sung before noon on week-days during Lent?*

Because, formerly, the faithful ate but once a day in Lent, and this was after Vespers, that is, around five or six o'clock in the evening. When the Church permitted the hour of the meal to be advanced, she likewise advanced the hour of Vespers; and since today the first meal is tolerated around midday, Vespers are for this reason sung before noon.[10]

474. *Is there anything else particular to Lent?*

There is also evening prayer, held two or three times a week, or even daily in many parishes.

475. *How is this exercise performed?*

The evening prayer is ordinarily recited in the vernacular; hymns are sung, and there is always a sermon. Then follows the *Miserere* or some other penitential chant, according to the custom of the parish, and most often the exercise concludes with Benediction of the Blessed Sacrament and the singing of the *Parce Domine*.

476. *Why are instructions more frequent during Lent?*

It is to remind the faithful of their religious obligations and to dispose them more fittingly to fulfill their Easter duty.

477. *How ought a Christian child to conduct himself during Lent?*

---

[10] The 1960 rubrics suppressed the requirement that Vespers in Lent be said before the main meal of the day and mandated instead that Vespers in Lent be said after noon.

He ought to redouble his piety, diligence in work, and obedience, and go to confession at the beginning of Lent, so as to prepare to do so again during Holy Week or the octave of Easter.

478. *What is the name of the fifth Sunday of Lent?*
It is called Passion Sunday.

479. *What notable thing takes place in the churches on that day?*
On the eve, before First Vespers of the Sunday, all the crosses and all the images of Our Lord, of the Blessed Virgin, and of the Saints are veiled in violet

480. *Why is this so?*
It is, first of all, as a sign of mourning and penance, because the time draws ever nearer when the Church is to celebrate the sufferings of Our Lord; and also because, during this same period, the Savior ceased to appear publicly to the people, according to these words of Saint John, which close the Gospel of Passion Sunday: "Jesus hid Himself and went out of the temple."

481. *Ought the crosses and images to be unveiled if a feast occurs?*
No, however solemn the feast may be.

482. *Before concluding the subject of Lent, tell us what are the other fast-days of the Christian year?*
They are the Vigils mentioned above, and the fast which the Church enjoins upon her children at the four seasons of the year (the Ember Days).

483. *At what time does each of these four fasts occur?*

They take place on Wednesday, Friday, and Saturday: for winter, in the week following the third Sunday of Advent; for spring, in the week of the First Sunday of Lent; for summer, during the octave of Pentecost; for autumn, in the week following the Exaltation of the Holy Cross (September 14).[11]

484. *What takes place on Ember Saturday?*

Priests and other ministers of the Church are ordained. On these days, Christians ought to pray for them in a most particular manner. — Ordinations may also take place on the eve of Passion Sunday and on Holy Saturday.[12]

§ VII.

FROM HOLY WEEK TO EASTER

OF HOLY WEEK IN GENERAL, AND PALM SUNDAY

485. *What is the name of the last week of Lent?*

It is called Holy Week, and in certain countries, the Great Week, or, as English Catholics say, the Good Week.

---

[11] Strictly speaking, the September Ember Days were assigned to the liturgical third week of September, which always fell after the fourteenth day of that month. In the 1960 reforms of the liturgy, the way the third week of September was calculated was changed, so that the Ember Days no longer necessarily fall on the week following the feast of the Exaltation of the Holy Cross.

[12] The 1983 Code of Canon Law (can. 1010) abolished the requirement that Ordinations take place on these days, instead assigning them to any Sunday or holy day of obligation, or, "for pastoral reasons," any other day.

486. *Why has it received this name?*
Because during this week the Church celebrates the mysteries of the Passion of Our Lord with solemn and imposing ceremonies, of a gravity and majesty uncommon in the year.

487. *How ought one to pass Holy Week?*
In piety, recollection, and penance.

488. *What is the first day of Holy Week?*
It is Palm Sunday.

489. *Why is it so called?*
Because at the procession that takes place before Mass, blessed palms or branches are carried.

490. *From what tree are the branches used in the procession taken?*
As nothing is prescribed in this regard, it varies according to the customs of different countries. In Rome, the Holy Father blesses true palm branches; in the south of France, olive branches are used; and in the north, branches of boxwood.

491. *Why has the Church instituted the procession of palms?*
To commemorate the triumphant entry of Our Lord into Jerusalem, amidst the people who bore palm branches and cast them upon His path.

492. *What is sung during this procession?*
Antiphons drawn from the Gospel are chanted, recalling the principal episodes of this triumph of the Savior.

493. *Where does the procession go?*

To a church, to a calvary,[13] or to the cemetery cross; sometimes the procession is made without any station [that is, a stop along the way].

494. *What happens upon the return from the procession?*

The door of the church is found to be closed.

495. *What is done then?*

The clergy and the faithful remain outside, and the choirboys sing within the church the hymn *Gloria, laus*, which the clergy and faithful repeat outside.

496. *Why is this hymn ordinarily sung within the church by children?*

To better represent the children who cried out in the temple: "Hosanna to the Son of David," which is recalled in this hymn.

497. *At what moment does one enter the church?*

When the hymn is finished, the subdeacon strikes the door of the church with the staff of the cross, whereupon it is immediately opened, and the procession enters the church chanting the responsory: *Ingrediente Domino*, etc.: "As the Lord entered the holy city, the children cried out Hosanna," etc.[14]

---

[13] That is, a crucifixion scene set up in the open or in a field.

[14] The reform of Holy Week in 1955 by Pius XII abolished the entrance ceremony described in nos. 494–98, making the *Gloria, laus* one of several possible processional chants while maintaining the *Ingrediente Domino* during the entering of the church.

498. *What is the meaning of this ceremony?*

It is to teach us that before the coming of Jesus Christ, the gate of Heaven was closed, and that it could only be opened to us by the merits of His Passion and of His Cross.

499. *With what dispositions ought one to be during the solemnity of Palm Sunday?*

One must unite oneself from the depths of the heart to the triumph of Our Lord, and ask Him for the grace not to imitate the Jews who, a few days after rendering Him such honors and expressing such admiration, crucified Him.

500. *What is particular about the Epistle of the Mass on Palm Sunday?*

It is that one kneels at the words: "In the name of Jesus every knee should bow, of those that are in Heaven, on earth, and under the earth."

501. *Why is this so?*

Because in that place, the Apostle Saint Paul says that at the name of Jesus every knee should bow, in Heaven, on earth, and under the earth.

502. *What is sung at Mass on Palm Sunday before the Gospel of the day?*

The Passion of Our Lord according to the Evangelist Saint Matthew is sung.[15]

---

[15] To be precise: the Gospel of the Mass, chanted by the deacon of the Mass and following more-or-less the usual ceremonies, comes *after* the chanting of the Passion; the two are separate, though contiguous. Historically, the Passion itself was never considered to be the Gospel of the Mass; it was made so only in Pius XII's Holy Week of 1955.

503. *And during the rest of the week?*

On Tuesday of Holy Week, the Passion according to Saint Mark is read; on Wednesday, the Passion according to Saint Luke; and on Good Friday, the Passion according to Saint John.

504. *What is particular about the singing of the Passion?*

It is chanted by three deacons: one takes the part of the Evangelist; the second sings all the words of Our Lord; and the third sings what is called the part of the Synagogue, that is, all the words of the Jews, of Pilate, etc.

505. *Have you noticed anything else during the singing of the Passion?*

Yes: when the deacon chants the passage of the Gospel which speaks of the Savior's last breath, everyone kneels on the ground and prays for the space of one *Pater noster*.

506. *Is it not customary to kiss the ground at that moment?*

Yes, in many places, especially in France; and it is a custom most worthy of praise, although not mentioned in the rubric. It is said that this practice originates with King Saint Louis, who once did so, which was an act imitated by the nobles of his court, and soon by all his subjects. The same is said of the words *Et incarnatus est* in the Creed.

507. *What else is particular about the singing of the Passion on Palm Sunday?*

It is that all in the choir who are not impeded by some liturgical duty, and all the faithful, are to bear palms in their hands.[16]

508. *What hymn is sung at Vespers on Palm Sunday?*

That day, as also on the preceding Sunday, the hymn *Vexilla Regis* is sung, which is a hymn of praise to the Cross.

509. *Why does everyone kneel at the strophe* O Crux, ave*?*

Because these words mean: "Hail, O Cross, our only hope," and the remainder of the strophe is no longer merely a praise, but a prayer to the Cross.

OF TENEBRAE AND MAUNDY THURSDAY

510. *What is the first office of the three great days of Holy Week?*

It is the Office of Tenebrae, which is celebrated on Wednesday evening, and likewise on the two following days.[17]

511. *Why are these Matins and Lauds called Tenebrae?*

In memory of ancient times, when they were chanted during the night.

512. *What is the color employed for this office?*

It is the color proper to the season of the Passion, violet.

---

[16] The holding of the blessed palms during the chanting of the Passion on Palm Sunday was suppressed by Pius XII.

[17] Pius XII moved the celebration of Tenebrae to the morning, the Masses to the evenings.

513. *What is notable about the Office of Tenebrae?*

It is the triangular candlestick upon which fifteen yellow wax candles burn, and which are extinguished one by one after each psalm.

514. *Whence comes this practice?*

It is a vestige of ancient usage. Since the office was very long, a large candlestick was placed in the midst of the choir, and the candles were extinguished as daylight increased.

515. *Why are these fifteen candles made of common yellow [i.e., unbleached] wax?*

As a sign of sorrow and mourning.

516. *Where is the triangular candlestick placed?*

On the Epistle side.

517. *What meaning may be given to the ceremony of extinguishing the candles?*

It has been said that the candles, extinguished one by one, represent the Apostles abandoning Our Lord one after another; and that the last candle, which remains alone and is hidden behind the altar, to be brought forth again at the end of the office, represents Our Lord disappearing shortly from the midst of men and reappearing, full of glory and light, in His Resurrection.[18]

518. *What else is noteworthy in the Office of Tenebrae?*

The Lamentations of Jeremiah.

---

[18] This ceremony was suppressed by Pius XII in 1955.

519. *What do you mean by this?*

They are the first three Lessons of the Office of Tenebrae. They are chanted in a mournful tone, to express the sorrow of the Church during the days of the death of the Savior.

520. *Why does the officiant make a slight noise at the end of Tenebrae?*

It is not only to signify that the office is ended, but also to recall the disorder of nature, something even more vividly represented in those places where it is the custom for everyone to repeat this noise with their book or upon the stalls.[19]

521. *What is the character of the offices of these last days?*

It is one of deep sorrow, and the thought of penance is incessantly mingled with that of the Passion of Jesus Christ.

522. *What is the prayer by which every Hour of the Divine Office concludes on these three days?*

It is the psalm *Miserere,* for during these holy days we cannot ask too often for the pardon of our sins.[20]

523. *What mystery does the Church celebrate on Holy Thursday?*

The institution of the sacrament of the Eucharist.

---

[19] The *strepitus* at the end of Tenebrae was suppressed by Pius XII in 1955.

[20] The recitation of the *Miserere* at the end of each Hour of the Office was suppressed by Pius XII in 1955.

524. *What is the ceremony that commemorates this great mystery?*

It is the Solemn Mass, the only Mass offered on that day. What distinguishes it is that all priests other than the celebrant, being unable to offer Mass, assist vested in stole or even in chasuble, and receive Holy Communion from the hand of the celebrant, who ought regularly to be the Superior of the place.

525. *What does this ceremony represent?*

This ceremony represents Our Lord Jesus Christ surrounded by His Apostles, to whom He gave Communion with His own hand at the Last Supper, which was the first of all Masses.

526. *What ceremony represents still more perfectly the Last Supper of Jesus Christ with His Apostles?*

To witness this ceremony one must go to the cathedrals. It is the blessing of the holy oils, in which the bishop is seated at a table in the midst of the choir, surrounded by twelve priests all vested in white chasubles, and by seven deacons and seven subdeacons clad in their ornaments of the same color.[21]

527. *What, then, are these oils consecrated by the bishop on Maundy Thursday?*

There are three kinds: (1) The OIL OF CATE-CHUMENS, used for baptism, the consecration of priests and bishops, and the blessing of bells; (2)

---

[21] This ceremony was modified and simplified by Pius XII, who promulgated an independent Chrism Mass, during which the oils are blessed. Previously, the blessing of oils occurred during the Mass of Holy Thursday.

The **HOLY CHRISM**, used for baptism, confirmation, the anointing of kings, and the consecration of churches, chalices, patens, etc.;[22] (3) The **OIL OF THE SICK**, which, as its name indicates, is used for the administration of extreme unction.

528. *What is further noteworthy in the Mass of Maundy Thursday?*

It is the Paschal Communion, which devout faithful prefer to make on this day, when possible.

529. *With what sentiments ought a Christian child to contemplate this august ceremony?*

By stirring within himself the desire to attain that blessedness, and by beseeching God for the grace to remain faithful throughout his life to his Easter duty. If he has already made his First Communion, he ought to prepare himself to kneel that very day at the Holy Table.

530. *How is the Mass sung?*

With great solemnity and with the usual signs of joy, yet not without certain differences that still mark the sorrow of the day.

531. *Can you cite a few examples?*

The Alleluia is not sung, and the crosses and images remain veiled; the cross of the high altar alone is covered during the Mass with a white veil placed over the customary violet one; the organ falls silent after the *Gloria in excelsis*, and the kiss of peace is omitted, owing to the horror the Church feels for the kiss of the traitor Judas.

---

[22] Chrism is also used in the consecration of bishops.

532. *What is particular about the* **Gloria in excelsis?**

All the bells of the church are rung aloud in joyful peal, and thereafter fall silent in token of sorrow, until the Mass of Holy Saturday.

533. *What is done after Communion?*

A consecrated host, placed in a chalice, is carried in great solemnity to the Altar of Repose, where it is to remain until the Mass of Good Friday.[23]

534. *At what moment is the sacred ciborium carried to the place of reservation?*

During Vespers.[24]

535. *How is Vespers recited?*

With lights, but without chant.[25]

536. *What is done after Vespers?*

The candles are extinguished, and the celebrant, accompanied by the deacon, subdeacon, and acolytes, strips the altars while the choir recites Psalm 21: *Deus, Deus meus, respice in me*, "My God, my God," etc., in which David foretells the circumstances of Our Lord's death, and His plaintive cry to the Father upon the Cross.[26]

---

[23] In Pius XII's Holy Week of 1955, a (full) ciborium with small hosts is carried, instead of a single consecrated celebrant's host.

[24] To be clear: the host for Good Friday is brought to the Altar of Repose, while the ciborium in the tabernacle is taken to the place of reservation during Vespers. In Pius XII's Holy Week of 1955, these separate actions are no longer needed, as all the hosts were brought to the Altar of Repose, not just one.

[25] In other words, entirely *recto tono.* These Vespers were suppressed by Pius XII in 1955.

[26] In Pius XII's Holy Week of 1955, the stripping of the altar happens immediately following Mass, which is then followed by Compline.

537. *What does this ceremony signify?*

It recalls the moment when the enemies of Our Lord, having stripped Him of His garments, divided them among themselves and cast lots for His robe. This is the meaning of the antiphon of the psalm just mentioned: *Diviserunt sibi vestimenta mea*, etc.

538. *What is, finally, the last ceremony of Maundy Thursday?*

It is the WASHING OF THE FEET.[27]

539. *Of what does this ceremony consist?*

It consists of washing the feet of twelve poor men, in remembrance of what Jesus Christ did on the eve of His death, when He washed the feet of His twelve Apostles.

540. *Who washes the feet of the poor?*

In each church, it is the superior of the place; at Rome, it is the pope; in the cathedral, the bishop; and in the parish, the parish priest.

541. *Why is it always the superior who washes the feet of the poor?*

Because Jesus Christ, who was God, and therefore superior to every creature, did not fear to give this example of humility.

542. *Could you tell us how the washing of feet is performed?*

---

[27] This ceremony occurred outside of and after Mass, with the Gospel of the Mass being repeated. In 1955, an option was given for performing this ceremony during the Mass after the Gospel.

The celebrant, following the example of Our Lord, girds himself with a towel, and after the chanting of the Gospel which recounts this final act of the Savior, he washes the feet of twelve children or elderly men, dries them, and kisses them, and often even gives alms to each one, when they are poor.

543. *What takes place on the evening of Holy Thursday and Good Friday?*

The Tenebrae, as on Wednesday; and towards evening, in many places, a sermon and the singing of the *Stabat Mater* at the Altar of Repose.

544. *What is the purpose of singing the* Stabat Mater?

It is to honor the sorrows of the Blessed Virgin at the foot of the Cross, and to weep with her over the death of her divine Son, our Savior.[28]

545. *What pious practices ought devout Christians to cherish on these two days?*

They ought, if they are able, to attend the morning offices [i.e., the solemn liturgies of Holy Thursday and Good Friday], to visit the Altar of Repose during the day,[29] and to make the Way of the Cross.

---

[28] The *Stabat Mater,* as a liturgical sequence, was suppressed by the Council of Trent (1545–1563) but restored to the missal in 1727 by Benedict XIII (1724–1730) for the Feast of the Seven Dolours of the Blessed Virgin Mary.

[29] Prior to Pius XII's Holy Week reform in 1955, the Holy Thursday and Good Friday liturgies would occur in the morning, allowing time during the day on Thursday to visit the Altar of Repose, which would remain accessible to the faithful until the beginning of the Good Friday liturgy. The Blessed

546. *What is the Way of the Cross?*

It is a devotion which consists in making, on one's knees, certain reflections upon the Passion of the Savior, at fourteen stations usually indicated in churches by pictures or small crosses. The manner of making it is explained in little booklets written expressly for this purpose, and even in the parish prayer-books.

OF GOOD FRIDAY

547. *What is the day of the year on which the ceremonies of the Church are most solemn and most sorrowful?*

It is Good Friday.

548. *What first strikes the eye upon entering the church on this day?*

It is that the altar is entirely stripped of its accustomed ornaments, the lamps and candles are extinguished, the tabernacle is open, and the bells are not rung.

549. *With what solemn ceremony does the Office of Good Friday begin?*

The celebrant and the ministers of the altar prostrate themselves, face to the ground, in the sanctuary upon the steps of the altar, and pray in silence for the space of a *Miserere*, while the rest of the choir, kneeling, likewise prays with heads bowed low.

Sacrament remained at the Altar of Repose until it was required on Good Friday. The Altar of Repose was then taken down after the Good Friday liturgy.

550. *What does this prayer and this profoundly humbled posture recall to us?*

It is that we cannot better commence the Office of so mournfully solemn a day than by being confounded at the sight of our sins and humbly imploring God's pardon.

551. *After this prostration, how does the Office continue?*

It begins with lessons, with prayers during which one kneels, and with tracts; then follows shortly the chanting of the Passion according to Saint John and its accompanying Gospel (at which neither candlesticks nor incense are brought), and finally the prayers known as the *Monitions* or the Solemn Orations.

552. *Why do you call them by that name?*

Because each of these prayers is preceded by an *admonition*, in which the priest declares the intention of the prayer about to be chanted.

553. *What takes place after the monitions?*

The priest sings *Oremus*, "Let us pray." The deacon immediately sings: *Flectamus genua*, "Let us kneel." Then all kneel, and rise again when the subdeacon sings *Levate*, "Arise."[30]

554. *What do you observe in these prayers?*

It is that the Church prays therein for the whole Church, and even for heretics, infidels, and Jews, something the Church does publicly only on Good Friday, to show that Jesus Christ died for all men.

---

[30] Pius XII's Holy Week of 1955 re-assigns the *Levate* to the deacon.

555. *Is there anything remarkable in the prayer for the Jews?*

Yes, it is that immediately after the monition, the priest sings the prayer without saying *Oremus,* and the faithful do not kneel.[31]

556. *Why is this so?*

Doubtless because the Church has wished thereby to express the horror inspired by that dreadful mockery of the Jews, who, after placing upon the Savior's head a crown of thorns, bent the knee before Him, saying: *Ave, Rex Judæorum,* "Hail, King of the Jews."[32]

557. *What is the ceremony that follows the prayers just mentioned?*

It is the Adoration of the Cross, the most solemn ceremony of the day's Office.

558. *How is the Adoration of the Cross performed?*

The celebrant unveils the Cross not all at once, but in three stages: first the top, then the right arm of the crucifix, and finally the entire Cross.

559. *What does he do at the same time?*

At each unveiling, he elevates the Cross a little higher and advances in three stages to the

---

[31] In 1955, Pius XII added the *Oremus* and kneeling to this prayer. Four years later, John XXIII slightly changed its text, and it was entirely rewritten by Benedict XVI (2005–2013) in 2008.

[32] It may be noted that it was not the Jews but the Gentiles who are recorded in Scripture as having bent the knee in mockery of Our Lord (see Mt 27:27–31; Mk 15:16–20). Others say that the Jews in the Middle Ages mocked Christians on Good Friday by making satirical genuflections and that, in reaction, the Christians stopped genuflecting at the mention of their names. The matter is obscure.

middle of the altar; and each time, he sings the antiphon *Ecce lignum Crucis*, "Behold the wood of the Cross," raising his voice progressively.

560. *What does the choir do at that moment?*

The choir, which stands during the antiphon *Ecce lignum*, responds when the priest has finished the antiphon: *Venite, adoremus* ("Come, let us adore"), in the same tone as the celebrant; at the same time, all, except the priest, bend both knees before the cross, then rise again, except on the final occasion, when all remain kneeling.

561. *What is done next?*

When the choir has sung *Venite, adoremus* for the third time, the celebrant places the cross upon a violet cushion laid on the footpace of the altar, on the Gospel side;[33] then, having removed his shoes — along with the deacon and subdeacon — they proceed to adore the cross, making at intervals three genuflections (going on both knees and bowing a little each time), then kissing the feet of the crucifix. The choir and all the faithful then do the same in turn.

562. *What is sung during the Adoration of the Cross?*

The antiphons called the *Improperia* are sung.

563. *What do you mean by the word* improperia?

It is a word derived from Latin meaning "reproaches," for these antiphons are composed

---

[33] The famous rubricist Martinucci states (in a book published in 1879) that the cross is placed on a cushion in the middle, which is where it will always be seen today.

of the reproaches which God, through His prophets, addressed to the Jewish people for their ingratitude.

564. *With what dispositions ought one to present oneself for the Adoration of the Cross?*

With sentiments of reverence and love for that sacred wood upon which Our Lord willed to be affixed for our sins, and with sincere contrition, remembering that our sins alone were the cause of His sufferings.

565. *In what posture ought the faithful to present themselves for the Adoration of the Cross?*

With arms crossed upon the breast, and with a profoundly recollected exterior.

566. *What is the ceremony which follows the Adoration of the Cross?*

It is the procession to the Altar of Repose, where the Host consecrated on the previous day is taken up.

567. *Why does one chant the* Vexilla Regis *while bringing the Sacred Host, and not the* Pange lingua, *as on the preceding day?*

Doubtless because the Church honors especially on this day the Cross upon which the Savior was affixed, and, in her deep sorrow, dares not intone a joyous and triumphant hymn such as the *Pange lingua.*

568. *What is the Mass of Good Friday called?*

It is called the Mass of the *Presanctified*, that is, of the gifts consecrated beforehand.

569. *Then does the priest not consecrate the Body of Our Lord at this Mass?*

No, he communicates only, and under one species alone, with a Host consecrated on Holy Thursday.

570. *Why is this so?*

Because the Church has judged that the commemoration of the great Sacrifice accomplished on this day suffices to enkindle the piety of the faithful, without the need of offering anew the Sacrifice of the Altar, which is its figure and its continuation.

571. *May one receive Communion on Good Friday?*

No, the clergy and faithful do not receive Communion on this day, except for the sick in danger of death.[34]

572. *How are Vespers said on Good Friday?*

They are recited without chant or light, no doubt to teach us that the Light of the World (Jesus Christ) has just been extinguished upon the Cross, leaving us all too much reason to weep over our sins.[35]

573. *Is there not also a sermon on Good Friday?*

Yes, one may say that in nearly all churches, on that day, the Passion of Our Lord is preached.[36]

---

[34] In 1955, general communion was introduced into the Good Friday liturgy.

[35] In 1955, these Vespers were suppressed.

[36] At the time of this writing, this sermon was usually said outside of the Mass of the Presanctified.

574. *What hour of Good Friday ought to be held in the greatest reverence?*

Three o'clock in the afternoon, because, according to the account of the Evangelists, it is the hour at which Our Lord died upon the Cross.

575. *What may one do to sanctify it?*

Among other devotions, one may go to church to pray or to make the Way of the Cross.[37]

OF HOLY SATURDAY

576. *With what ceremony does the Office of Holy Saturday begin?*

With the blessing of the new fire.

577. *Why is there no fire in the church, and why are all the lamps extinguished?*

It is to represent that the Light of the world, Jesus Christ, hidden in the tomb, ought not to shine before the eyes of men until His Resurrection, the Vigil of which is now beginning to be celebrated.

578. *Where is the new fire blessed?*

At the door of the church, and a portion of it is placed in a thurible.

579. *What is done next?*

As all present process into the church, the triple-branched candle, affixed to the end of a reed, is lighted three times, each time with a

---

[37] Prior to Pius XII's Holy Week of 1955, the Liturgy of Good Friday would have been celebrated in the morning. With Tenebrae in the evening, the afternoon was free for such devotions.

genuflection. As the deacon who carries it kindles each of the three flames, he sings, raising his voice each time: *Lumen Christi*: "The Light of Christ." At these words, the choir responds thrice likewise, in the same tone as the deacon: *Deo gratias*.[38]

580. *What is done upon arrival at the sanctuary?*

The deacon blesses the Paschal Candle by chanting the beautiful canticle known as the *Exsultet*, so called from its opening word.[39]

581. *What is the Paschal Candle?*

It is a large and noble candle of white wax, which is blessed each year on Holy Saturday, to be lighted during all the ceremonies of the Paschal season.

582. *What does the Paschal Candle represent?*

It represents Jesus Christ, already resplendent with glory upon earth after His Resurrection. The Church, in the *Exsultet*, likens it to the pillar of fire which led the Hebrews by night through the desert and delivered them from Egyptian bondage.

583. *What do the five grains of incense affixed in the form of a cross to the Paschal Candle represent?*

They represent the five sacred wounds of the Savior, as well as the aromatic spices with which His Body was embalmed.[40]

---

[38] In 1955, Pius XII suppressed the use of this triple-branched candle. The Paschal Candle is lit directly from the new fire and blessed before entering the church.

[39] Pius XII's Holy Week of 1955 removed the prayers of blessing from the text of the *Exsultet*.

[40] In 1955, the insertion of incense grains into the Paschal Candle was moved prior to its lighting and blessing.

584. *What follows after the* Exsultet*?*

Lectors chant twelve lengthy lessons called the prophecies, in which are set forth the miseries of man following his fall, and the promise of his deliverance through the power of Jesus Christ.[41]

585. *What ceremony follows these prophecies?*

It is the blessing of the water of the baptismal font.

586. *Why is this water blessed on Holy Saturday?*

It is blessed on Holy Saturday and on the Vigil of Pentecost,[42] because formerly it was only on these two days that solemn baptism was conferred. This is in memory of that ancient custom.

587. *Is there not, in connection with this ceremony, a very widespread custom in the parishes?*

Yes, it is the pious custom of receiving the aspersion of the baptismal water before the priest has mingled with it the holy oils and the sacred chrism, thus recalling the solemn baptism which the bishop formerly administered on this holy day to a great multitude of catechumens.[43]

---

[41] In 1955, the number of prophecies was reduced to four.

[42] In 1955, the blessing of the water for the font on the Vigil of Pentecost was abolished.

[43] There are two types of water blessed during the Easter (and Pentecost) Vigil in the baptistry. The first can be called lustral or Easter (Pentecost) water. Some of this water is removed from the large container near the baptismal font and then placed into the font itself (or a container in the font). To the water in the font is added the oils. The smaller amount to which the oils were added is the baptismal water. It is the first water, the lustral or Easter (Pentecost) water, which is used to sprinkle the faithful and which the faithful can take home with them. The second water is reserved strictly for the celebration of baptism.

588. *How ought one to assist at the blessing of the baptismal font?*

By recalling the promises of one's own baptism and renewing them from the depths of the heart.[44]

589. *Ought one to have a particular devotion to the holy water blessed on Holy Saturday?*

It is a most laudable practice, and devout Christians are eager to have some in their homes; for this reason, in all parishes, a large quantity is blessed.

590. *What is done when the blessing is completed?*

The procession returns to the choir while chanting a litany, and upon arrival, all kneel. After this, the Mass begins with the singing of the *Kyrie*.

591. *Why is there no Introit in the Mass of Holy Saturday?*

Because the Introit marks the entrance of the priest to the altar, and it is unnecessary here, since the celebrant has already been present for a long time for the preceding ceremonies. The final litany, sung upon re-entering the choir, takes its place.

592. *What is the second particularity of the Mass of Holy Saturday?*

It is that during the *Gloria in excelsis*, all the bells are rung, to express the great joy to which the Church is already beginning to give voice in the offices of the Eve of the Resurrection,[45] and

---

[44] A public renewal of baptismal promises was added to the ceremony of the Easter Vigil in Pius XII's 1955 Holy Week.

[45] It should be noted that the Easter Vigil Mass, while is partakes in an overflow, as it were, of the joy of the next day, is not a Mass of Easter properly speaking. The Mass of the Easter Vigil is just that, a *Vigil* Mass. It is not the "First Mass

to summon the faithful to the first chanting of the *Alleluia*, which the priest is about to intone. It is also at the *Gloria in excelsis* that, in Rome, the veils are removed from the statues and the images of the saints.

593. *What is the third particularity of this Mass?*

It is the chanting of the Alleluia at the Gradual. The celebrant intones it a first time, and the choir repeats it on the same tone. The celebrant then sings it a second time, higher, and a third time, higher still, which the choir likewise repeats.

594. *How are the First Vespers of the feast of Easter sung?*

They are sung after the Communion of the Holy Saturday Mass. They are very brief, consisting only of the short psalm *Laudate Dominum omnes gentes* and the *Magnificat*, with their antiphons, which are doubled. The altar is incensed during the *Magnificat*. Vespers end with the Post-Communion of the Mass and the chanting of the *Ite missa est*, to which the deacon adds two alleluias. The choir, in turn, responds *Deo gratias, alleluia, alleluia*, a practice continued until the following Saturday inclusive, in sign of the Church's great joy.[46]

of Easter" in the way that the Midnight Mass is the First Mass of Christmas. It is, rather, the Mass proper to Holy Saturday, the Vigil Day.

[46] Due to the changes made by Pius XII in 1955, the First Vespers of Easter at the end of the Vigil Mass was replaced by Easter Lauds, consisting of Psalm 150 and the *Benedictus*. This also corresponded with the change of the time of the Easter Vigil, made by the same pontiff, to a much later time so that the Mass would begin around midnight, with the Vigil, then, starting around 10 pm. While it is true that the Vigil would anciently start around sunset, hence the lighting of the fire,

595. *What takes place in many churches toward evening?*

Compline and Matins of Easter are sung.[47]

§ VIII.
OF THE SUNDAY OF THE RESURRECTION (EASTER SUNDAY) AND THE EASTER SEASON

596. *What is the day of Easter?*

It is the Sunday of the Resurrection of Our Lord Jesus Christ.

597. *With what dispositions ought we to attend the offices of this great day?*

With sentiments of true gratitude toward our divine Redeemer and with a joy wholly sacred, since the Resurrection of the Savior is the pledge of our own resurrection.

598. *What do you observe in the whole of the Easter Day offices?*

It is the joy that bursts forth everywhere, in the words as in the songs of Holy Church: she

---

the idea that the ceremonies would begin so late and carry over into the next day does not have a strong historical foundation. In defense of the pre-1955 practice: as all feasts would historically start with First Vespers, this Vespers ceremony at the end of the Vigil Mass marked the actual start of the Feast of the Resurrection and more properly corresponded to the timing of a vigil/penitential Mass, which traditionally started in the late afternoon or early evening (the Easter Vigil was, of course, only one of many vigils in the Roman liturgy prior to Pius XII's alteration of the calendar). In the books of Paul VI, the start time of the Easter Vigil was moved to sunset-time.

[47] Due to the change of the timing of Easter Vigil and the corresponding change to the Vigil Mass by Pius XII in 1955, these are no longer observed except by those who do not attend the Vigil. As a result, these Hours are prayed in private.

repeats almost at every moment her cry of gladness: *Alleluia*.

599. *What does the procession held in many churches on Easter Day represent?*

It represents the journey of the holy women to the sepulcher, at the rising of the sun.

600. *What is the* O filii?*

The *O filii*, which is proper to Easter Week, as well as the sequence *Victimæ paschali laudes*, are two simple, touching, and joyful songs on the Resurrection of Our Lord.

601. *What is particular to the Easter season?*

It is that during the antiphon *Regina cœli*, one always remains standing, in memory of the Resurrection of the Savior; that there is no fasting, because of the joy proper to the season; and that in all the principal parts of the Office, such as the antiphons, responsories, and verses, one adds one or several *Alleluias*. — During Easter Week only, two are added to the *Benedicamus* at Lauds and Vespers, but not at the Little Hours.

602. *When does the Easter season end?*

The Easter season ends at First Vespers of the Feast of the Most Holy Trinity, that is, with the close of the week of Pentecost.

603. *How many Sundays are there after Easter?*

There are five, during which the Church has us read, in the Gospel of the Mass, passages taken for the most part from the discourse of Our Lord after the Last Supper.

§ IX.
OF THE ROGATION DAYS
AND THE ASCENSION

604. *Are there not processions between Easter and the Ascension?*

Yes, the processions of Saint Mark and of the three days of the Rogation.

605. *What is sung during these processions?*

The Litany of the Saints is chanted.

606. *What does the word* Rogation *mean?*

It is as though one was saying prayers.

607. *What is the purpose of these processions?*

It is to draw down the blessings of God upon the fruits of the earth, and to beseech Him to preserve us from scourges such as pestilence, lightning, or war.

608. *What else do these processions bring to mind?*

That we are but pilgrims upon the earth.

609. *Is abstinence observed during these four days?*

Yes, unless a dispensation be granted by the bishop, which he sometimes does by the authority of the Sovereign Pontiff.

610. *What is the Ascension?*

It is the first great feast that follows Easter, and it commemorates the day on which Our Lord ascended in glory into Heaven, forty days after His Resurrection.

611. *What is particular to this day?*

It is that, at the Gospel, after the words *Assumptus est in cælum*, "He was taken up into Heaven," the Paschal Candle is extinguished.[48]

612. *Why is this done?*

Because the Paschal Candle is the figure of Jesus Christ; and this ceremony reminds the faithful that this divine Savior, having dwelt among men for forty days after His Resurrection, has now withdrawn from their sight.[49]

§ X.
FROM PENTECOST TO ADVENT

613. *What is the great feast that follows the Ascension?*

It is Pentecost, when the Church celebrates the descent of the Holy Ghost upon the Apostles. — It is, after Easter, the greatest feast of the Christian year.

614. *What is to be said of the Vigil of this solemnity?*

That on this day the blessing of the baptismal fonts takes place, as on Holy Saturday.[50]

---

[48] And, after the Mass, the Candle is removed from the Church. After this time, the Paschal Candle is not used again liturgically except on the Vigil of Pentecost to bless the water.

[49] The Feast of the Ascension is celebrated with an octave of privileged Paschal days, and then with thirty-three days that have paschal character. On the fortieth day the faithful celebrate the ascension of Christ into Heaven, and on the fiftieth day they celebrate the descent of the Holy Spirit upon the Apostles at Pentecost. Ascensiontide, therefore, is that ten-day period between the Ascension and Pentecost. Inasmuch as nine days of prayer precede the outpouring of the Holy Spirit, it is regarded as the first novena.

[50] This blessing, together with the reading of prophecies, was suppressed by Pius XII in 1955.

615. *What does the word Pentecost mean?*

It means "fiftieth day," because this feast is celebrated fifty days after Easter.

616. *What is the particular ceremony of this day?*

The Roman rubric prescribes none; yet one ought to have a special devotion to assist, on this day, at the Hour of Terce in those churches where it is sung, as for example in cathedrals.

617. *Why is this so?*

Because, according to the account given in Holy Scripture, it was at the Hour of Terce that the Holy Ghost descended upon the Apostles.

618. *What hymn is sung at Terce on the day of Pentecost?*

The *Veni Creator* is sung, as also at Vespers and likewise throughout the Octave, in order to implore the Holy Ghost to descend into our souls. The first stanza is sung on one's knees.

619. *What do you know concerning the Octave of Pentecost?*

It is privileged, and concludes, like the Octave of Easter, after None on the Saturday.

620. *What is the feast that follows this Octave?*

It is the feast of the Most Holy Trinity, the solemnity of which offers nothing particular.

621. *How many Sundays are there after Pentecost?*

There are from twenty-three to twenty-eight, according as Easter has fallen earlier or later. When there are more than twenty-four, the Sundays whose

Offices could not be celebrated after the Epiphany are resumed.

622. *What is the feast that follows the Octave of Pentecost?*

It is the feast of the Most Blessed Sacrament, commonly called **CORPUS CHRISTI**.[51] It is celebrated on the Thursday following Trinity Sunday; but in France, the outward solemnity is deferred to the following Sunday. — In certain churches, the Thursday of the feast of the Blessed Sacrament is chosen, preferably, for the celebration of First Communion, and this is a holy and beautiful custom.

623. *What is most noteworthy in this feast?*

It is the solemn procession of the Blessed Sacrament.

624. *How is this procession performed?*

It is performed with great solemnity. The celebrant, vested in a white cope, bears the Most Holy Eucharist beneath a canopy. The Blessed Sacrament is escorted with torches and smoking

---

[51] The visions of St. Juliana of Liège (1192/3-1258) inspired the Feast of Corpus Christi to honor the Real Presence of Christ in the Eucharist. With the support of Archdeacon Jacques Pantaléon, the feast was first celebrated at Fosses in the Diocese of Liège in 1246. In 1264, a year after the Miracle of Bolsena, Pantaléon, now Urban IV (1261-1264), officially instituted Corpus Christi as a feast in the Church via the bull *Transiturus de hoc mundo*. At the Council of Vienne (1311-1312), Clement V (1305-1314) included the bull of Urban IV in the collection of laws known as the *Clementine Constitutions* that would be promulgated by John XXII (1316-1334) in 1317, universally establishing the Feast of Corpus Christi for the entire Church. John XXII also introduced an octave and procession of the Blessed Sacrament in 1318.

thuribles. — Often, little choir children carry baskets of flowers and strew them in the path of Our Lord. Along the route of the procession, the houses are adorned with hangings, and the ways are strewn with flowers and greenery. One or two altars of repose are prepared along the way, and it is at these, after the singing of the *Tantum ergo* and the customary incensations, that the priest gives the faithful Benediction with the Blessed Sacrament.

625. *What was the Church's intention in instituting this feast?*

It is to honor Our Lord in a special manner in the sacrament of His love, and to make reparation for the outrages He receives in the Most Holy Eucharist.

626. *What ought one to do in order to enter into the Church's intention?*

One ought to contribute, as far as one is able, to the adornment of the streets and the altars of repose, and to follow the procession with profound reverence and great devotion.

627. *What are the particular features of the Octave of Corpus Christi?*

From the Thursday of Corpus Christi to the Thursday of the Octave, in many churches the Blessed Sacrament remains exposed from the first Mass until Benediction at dusk. In large churches, both the Mass and Vespers are sung before the exposed Blessed Sacrament. In smaller churches and parish churches where there would not be adorers, it is exposed only during the Mass, and Benediction is sung.[52]

628. *What is the final feast of the Proper of Time before Advent?*

It is the anniversary of the dedication of all churches, or the Feast of the Dedication.[53]

629. *What pious thought ought we to draw from this feast?*

We ought to reflect that, like the churches built of stone, our bodies have been consecrated to be temples of the Holy Ghost, and we should renew the promises made on the day of our baptism, to belong to God forever.

---

[52] The Octave of Corpus Christi was suppressed by Pius XII in 1955.

[53] This seems to be a feast proper to France.

CHAPTER III

✠

The Common and the Proper of Saints

630. *How do you divide the Proper of Saints?*

It may be divided into three classes of feasts: (1) the feasts of the Blessed Virgin; (2) the feasts of the Angels; (3) the feasts of the Saints.

631. *What is the general intention of the Church in instituting these feasts?*

Her intention is to cause us to admire, celebrate, and imitate the virtues of the Blessed Virgin and of the saints, things which redound to the glory of God and to the salvation of our souls.

632. *What do you first observe concerning the Blessed Virgin?*

It is that, whereas the greatest saints have but one or two feast days, the Church celebrates each year a great number in honor of the Blessed Virgin.

633. *Can you give a reason for this practice of the Church?*

It is her admiration for the virtues of the Blessed Virgin and her tender affection for that good Mother, which stirs the Church's zeal to celebrate, by so many feasts, the virtues and privileges of the Mother of God.

634. *What are the principal feasts of the Blessed Virgin as listed in the Roman Calendar?*

They are, beginning with Advent: the Immaculate Conception of the Blessed Virgin (December 8); the Purification (February 2);[1] the Annunciation (March 25); the Visitation (July 2); the Assumption (August 15); the Nativity of the Blessed Virgin (September 8); and the Presentation in the Temple (November 21).

635. *What is the feast of the Immaculate Conception?*

It is a feast in which the Church honors the glorious privilege by which the Blessed Virgin was preserved, from the first instant of her existence, from the stain of original sin, with which we are all born defiled as children of Adam.

636. *Is this feast very ancient?*

The feast of the Conception is very ancient, but the feast of the Immaculate Conception has been celebrated throughout the entire Church only since December 8, 1854, when our Holy Father Pope Pius IX, by his apostolic authority, proclaimed Mary, Immaculate in her Conception, and made this holy belief a dogma of faith for all Christians.

637. *What is the Purification?*

It is a feast wherein the Church celebrates the obedience and humility of the Blessed Virgin, who presented herself in the temple according to the Law, like the other women of Israel, forty days after the birth of Our Lord.

638. *What is the feast of the Annunciation?*

On this feast, the Church recalls the day when

---

[1] Curiously, although its name remains the same, this feast was categorized as a feast of the Lord by John XXIII in the 1962 missal.

the Archangel Gabriel came to announce to the Blessed Virgin that she would become the Mother of the Son of God, the Savior of men.

639. *What does the feast of the Visitation recall?*

It recalls the charitable visit which the Blessed Virgin made to Saint Elizabeth, the mother of Saint John the Baptist.

640. *What is the Assumption?*

The Assumption is the principal feast of the Blessed Virgin. On this day, the Church celebrates the triumph of that good Mother of God, who was taken up into Heaven by the angels and placed at the right hand of her divine Son.

641. *Does France not observe a particular solemnity on that day?*

Yes, it is the procession of the vow of Louis XIII, who consecrated to the Blessed Virgin his person, his family, and his kingdom. In fulfillment of that vow, a procession is held throughout France after Vespers, during which the Litany of the Blessed Virgin is chanted.

642. *What is the Nativity?*

It is the feast of the anniversary of the birth of the Most Blessed Virgin.

643. *What is the Presentation of the Blessed Virgin?*

It is a feast on which the Church commemorates the consecration which the Blessed Virgin made of herself to the Lord in the temple of Jerusalem, at the age of three years, promising to remain ever a virgin.

644. *What are the other feasts of the Blessed Virgin?*

There are many throughout the year. — These include: on December 10, the Translation of the Holy House of the Blessed Virgin, which the angels transported from Nazareth to Loreto; on December 18, the Expectation of the Divine Childbirth of the Blessed Virgin; on January 23, the Marriage of the Blessed Virgin with Saint Joseph; on May 24, the feast of Our Lady Help of Christians. — We invoke the Blessed Virgin on this feast under the title *Auxilium Christianorum*, "Help of Christians." On July 9, the feast of the Miracles of the Blessed Virgin; on the 16th of the same month, Our Lady of Mount Carmel, or the feast of the Holy Scapular; on August 5, the Dedication of Our Lady of the Snows in Rome; on the Sunday following the Nativity, the feast of the Holy Name of Mary;[2] on the third Sunday of September, the feast of the Seven Sorrows of the Blessed Virgin at the foot of the Cross, which had already been celebrated on the Friday of Passion Week;[3] on September 24, Our Lady of Ransom. Then follow the feasts of the four Sundays in October, namely, the feasts of the Holy Rosary, the Maternity of the Blessed Virgin, her Purity, and her Patronage.[4] Most of these are celebrated by papal privilege.[5]

---

[2] In 1911, Pius X fixed this feast to September 12.

[3] In 1911, Pius X fixed this feast to September 15.

[4] In 1911, Pius X fixed these first three feasts to October 7, 11, and 16, respectively. The feast of the Patronage was eliminated from most local calendars, and if kept it was assigned to various days.

[5] Of these, the following are included in the 1961 universal calendar promulgated by John XXIII: Our Lady of Sorrows on Passion Friday (reduced to a commemoration), Our Lady of Mount Carmel (reduced to a commemoration), Our Lady

645. *With what dispositions ought we to celebrate the feasts of the Blessed Virgin?*

With sentiments of tender confidence in the power of this glorious Queen of angels and of men, and of tender love toward our good Mother.

646. *What are the feasts of the angels?*

They are: (1) the feasts of the three archangels: Saint Michael, who vanquished the rebellious angel (September 29); Saint Gabriel, who announced to Mary the mystery of the Incarnation (March 18); and Saint Raphael, who guided Tobias (October 24); (2) the feast of all the holy Guardian Angels (October 2).

647. *What ought we to ask on these feasts?*

We ought to beseech the holy angels to deign to offer our prayers to God and to serve as our guides on the great journey to Heaven.

648. *How many orders of saints does the Roman Church count?*

The Roman Breviary counts five principal orders: the Apostles, the Martyrs, the Confessors, the Virgins, and the Holy Women.

649. *What is meant by saying that the office is taken from the Common?*

This means that when a saint does not have a proper office, the office common to saints of

---

of the Snows, the Holy Name of Mary, the September feast of Our Lady of Sorrows, Our Lady of Ransom (reduced to a commemoration), Our Lady of the Rosary, and the Maternity of the Blessed Virgin Mary. Additionally, it includes the feast of the Immaculate Heart of the Blessed Virgin Mary (August 22), instituted in 1944, and of her Queenship (May 31), instituted in 1954.

his order is used to celebrate his feast; hence one speaks of the Common of Apostles, of Virgins, etc.

650. *What is an Apostle?*

The Church gives this name to those saints whom Our Lord Himself sent to preach the Gospel, either during His mortal life or after His Resurrection, as He did with Saint Paul, whom He called to Himself in a vision on the road to Damascus, and Saint Barnabas.

651. *Who are the chief among the Apostles?*

They are Saint Peter and Saint Paul, who both, in Rome, sealed with their blood the faith of Jesus Christ, and whom the holy doctors have called the two pillars of the Church.

652. *How is their feast celebrated?*

With great solemnity, on the 29th of June.

653. *What are the Martyrs?*

They are all the saints who shed their blood and gave their lives in witness to their faith in Jesus Christ.

654. *Which of the holy martyrs are specially honored by the Church?*

They are Saint Stephen, the first martyr; and Saint Lawrence, deacon of the Roman Church, who was burned alive.

655. *Who are the Confessors?*

The Church gives this name to all the holy men — bishops, priests, religious, or lay faithful — who, without suffering death for the faith, practiced its Christian virtues in a heroic manner throughout their lives.

656. *Which of the holy Confessors are specially distinguished in the Church's cultus?*

They are Saint Joseph, spouse of the Blessed Virgin, and Saint Martin, whose sanctity and miracles shone forth with great splendor.

657. *Who are the Virgins?*

They are the holy women who consecrated their lives to God in chastity and who never entered the bonds of marriage. The Church distinguishes in her offices between virgins and virgin-martyrs.

658. *Which are the most highly honored holy virgins in the Church?*

They are Saint Agnes, Saint Agatha, Saint Lucy, and Saint Cecilia, whose names are inscribed in the Canon of the Mass.

659. *Which saints are included under the name of holy women?*

They are those who were sanctified in the holy state of matrimony or in widowhood, whether they suffered martyrdom or not.

660. *What is the greatest feast of the saints?*

It is All Saints' Day, or the Feast of All Saints, in which the Church sings the praises of the Church Triumphant in its entirety, and invokes it with one and the same prayer.

661. *What solemnity is celebrated on the day following All Saints?*

It is the Commemoration of All the Faithful Departed. The only proper feature is the Office of the Dead, which is sometimes sung in its entirety in the morning.[6] (In many places, after the Gospel of the principal Mass, a priest ascends the pulpit and commends to the prayers of the faithful a great number of the departed whose names have been given to him; thereafter, the *De Profundis* is recited or sung, or else the Offertory is sung immediately, which is a very beautiful prayer for the dead.)

662. *With what sentiments ought a Christian to assist at this ceremony?*

With the thought that he himself may one day be detained for a long time in Purgatory, and that he will then rejoice that the faithful on earth pray for him; and in this thought, he ought to pray fervently for all the poor departed, and in particular for his deceased family and friends.

---

[6] Originally the Office of the Dead (Vespers, Matins, and Lauds) was said in addition to the Office of the day (the second day within the octave of All Saints). In 1911, Pius X promulgated a complete Office of the Dead to be said in place of the Office of the day within the octave.

# APPENDIX I

PONTIFICAL CEREMONIES

§ I.
OF THE PONTIFICAL OFFICE

663. *What are the Pontifical functions at which the faithful may have occasion to be present?*

They are: confirmation, the Pontifical Office, the Ordination of Priests and clerics, the Consecration of a bishop, the Consecration of a church or the laying of its cornerstone, the Consecration of an altar, the blessing of a cemetery, the blessing of a bell.

664. *What is meant by Pontifical Office?*

The name is given to those offices in which the bishop, or a prince of the Church possessing episcopal privileges, presides in all the splendour of pontifical majesty, vested in all the ornaments proper to his order.

665. *What is notable about the Pontifical Mass?*

(1) While the choir sings the Hour of Terce, the bishop is solemnly vested at his throne with all the ornaments of the episcopal order. (2) Throughout the function he is surrounded by the canons, or by a certain number of priests VESTED, that is, clothed in copes or chasubles, who come

before the throne to recite with him the *Gloria in excelsis* and the Creed after he has intoned them. (3) In addition to the deacon and subdeacon of the Mass, who are seated at the credence with the acolytes, there are **TWO ASSISTANT DEACONS** seated at the throne with the bishop, and an assistant priest in cope, to whom is entrusted the care of the book: it is he who points out to the bishop what he is to read or sing, and who holds the candle near the pontiff when he uses the book. It need hardly be added that when the pope pontificates, the functions we have just described are performed by cardinals. — Then the functions of acolytes, candle-bearers, and thurifers, which are ordinarily fulfilled near the bishop by priests or clerics, are performed by prelates of the Roman court: apostolic protonotaries, chamberlains, or others.

666. *Why is a seventh candle lit when the bishop pontificates?*

It is to represent the fullness of the seven gifts of the Holy Ghost which he received at his consecration and which he is charged to pour forth upon priests and upon the faithful, through Ordination and through confirmation.

667. *What is meant by a Pontifical Mass at the Faldstool, and what is its particular characteristic?*

It is the name given to a Mass celebrated pontifically by a bishop in a church or in circumstances where he does not have the right to a throne; for example, if he celebrates in the presence of the diocesan bishop who is assisting pontifically. — It is always thus for a cardinal or a bishop celebrating before the Sovereign Pontiff. — In such a case, the cardinal or bishop celebrating makes use of a chair without a back, which resembles a folding stool with arms. This chair is placed, without any platform, upon a carpet on the Epistle side, in such a manner that the bishop faces the people. The assistant priest, the deacon, and the subdeacon are seated on the bench; the other ministers remain standing near the celebrant or at the credence; they sit upon the steps of the altar if there is a sermon.

668. *What is meant by Pontifical Chapel?*

A bishop is said to HOLD CHAPEL when, not celebrating himself, he assists in cope, miter, and with the other episcopal insignia, at an office celebrated before him by a bishop or by a priest. The pope, who very rarely pontificates himself, on the contrary very frequently holds Papal Chapel.

669. *What are the particular features of pontifical Vespers?*

The faithful need only observe their great solemnity, the short chapter chanted before the bishop by the subdeacon of the Mass, and the blessing which concludes them. They will also note that, whereas in solemn Vespers the priests wear only the surplice (or the rochet, if they are canons) and the cope, the bishop is vested over the rochet with the amice, the alb, the cincture, the pectoral cross, the stole, the cope, and the miter.

§ II.
OF CONFIRMATION

670. *How ought the bishop to be received when he visits a parish of his diocese?*

At the entrance to the town, or at the place designated for receiving the prelate, a prie-Dieu is prepared upon a carpet. The superior of the place, vested in a precious cope over the surplice (or the rochet, if he is a canon), goes out to meet the bishop in procession; upon reaching him, he presents for his reverence the crucifix, which he must have brought from the church. The bishop then places himself beneath a canopy carried by the local notables; they proceed to the church singing the canticle *Benedictus Dominus Deus Israël*, "Blessed be the Lord God of Israel, for He has visited His people." Upon arrival at the church door, the superior presents him with holy water and incense, then greets him formally, if such be the custom. Thereafter they go to the altar, where the bishop kneels while the superior chants the versicles and the prayer for the bishop. The antiphon of the church's patron saint is also sung, after which the bishop ascends the altar and gives the solemn blessing.

671. *How ought one to comport oneself at the bishop's passing?*

One ought to kneel to receive his blessing.

672. *What is noteworthy in the ceremony of confirmation?*

Four circumstances are particularly noteworthy in this rite: (1) The **EXAMINATION** ordinarily made by the bishop himself or by his delegates, to ensure that the confirmands possess sufficient knowledge of the first truths of the Christian faith. (2) The **IMPOSITION OF HANDS**, by which he calls down upon them the seven gifts of the Holy Ghost. (3) The **ANOINTING WITH HOLY CHRISM**, by which he marks them on the forehead with the sign of the cross, that they may never blush for the crucified Jesus. (4) Finally, the recitation aloud of the Creed, the *Pater noster*, and the *Ave Maria*, which serves as an initiation of these newly "perfect Christians" into public prayer.

§ III.
OF ORDINATIONS

673. What general observation may be made concerning the ceremony of Ordination?

One ought to note that the conferral of each of the sacred orders comprises: (1) The **MONITIONS**, that is, admonitions in which the bishop sets forth to the ordinands the duties which the order they are to receive shall impose upon them; (2) The **PRAYERS**, that is, long supplications which the pontiff addresses to God, that those he is about to ordain may fulfill their functions worthily; (3) The **VESTURE**, that is, the moment when the bishop clothes the clerics with the ornaments proper to their order; (4) Finally, what might be called the **ENTHRONEMENT**, that is, the moment when the bishop causes each ordinand to touch the various objects to which his order entitles him, and which he is henceforth bound to use in the ministry of Jesus Christ.

674. *How does the bishop confer the tonsure?*

The new clerics, kneeling before him in cassock, receive from the pontiff the cutting of five locks of hair in the form of a cross; he then himself clothes them in the surplice. Finally, having taken his seat, he reminds the newly tonsured that they now belong to the clergy, and that they must strive to preserve its privileges by pure morals and an edifying life.

675. *What are the four minor orders?*

They are the orders of porter, lector, exorcist, and acolyte.

676. *How is the ordination of porters performed?*

All the clerics who are to receive this order kneel in surplice before the bishop, who, after the monition, causes them to touch with their right hand the keys of the church. Then the archdeacon leads them to the door of the church, which he makes them open and shut; after which he hands them the bell-rope that they may ring the bells, or at least a small bell that they may shake it. — Upon their return, the bishop recites a prayer in which he asks of God the graces necessary for the newly ordained to fulfill well their new functions. — This is the pattern we present once for all the orders.

677. *How is the ordination of lectors performed?*

The clerics who are to receive this order being placed as we have described in number 676 (which we shall not repeat, since it applies to all the orders), the bishop recites the monition, causes them to touch the **BOOK OF LESSONS**, and then recites the appropriate prayer.

678. *How is the ordination of exorcists performed?*

After the monition, the bishop causes the ordinands to touch the book of exorcisms, and then recites the prayer for those who have received this order.

679. *How is the ordination of acolytes performed?*

The order of acolytes is the last and highest of the minor orders, because those who receive it draw nearer to the holy altar during the august sacrifice. After the monition, the bishop causes the acolytes to touch a candlestick with a wax candle, to signify that they must carry and light the candles in the church. — He then causes them to touch an empty cruet, to teach them that they are to present the wine and water to the sacred ministers for the Holy Sacrifice of the Mass. Then he recites three prayers for the new acolytes. — This is the last order for which the clerics are vested in surplice.

680. *What are the three sacred orders?*

They are the subdiaconate, the diaconate, and the priesthood.

681. *What general remarks may be made regarding these three orders?*

(1) The ordinands are vested with the amice, alb, and cincture, and it is upon these garments that the bishop places the ornaments proper to their respective orders. (2) All are to receive Holy

Communion. (3) All clerics in these three orders perform the prostration; that is, at the command of the archdeacon, they lie prostrate, face to the ground, upon carpets, and remain so during the entire singing of the Litany of the Saints. — This solemn ceremony is found likewise in all consecrations of persons to the service of God: in the consecration of bishops, of kings and queens, in the blessing of abbots, abbesses, and virgins; and likewise at the blessing of the first stone of a church, at its dedication, and at the blessing of a cemetery by the bishop.

682. *How is the ordination of subdeacons performed?*

The bishop begins with a first monition in which he reminds the future subdeacons of the obligations they are about to assume. — He concludes it with these words: "And if you persevere in your good desire to consecrate yourselves to God, in the name of the Lord, draw near." At that moment, all the subdeacons take a step toward the altar, to mark their will to consummate their sacrifice. (If the subdeacons are all religious, the bishop omits this first monition, as they have already made their vows.) Then are called those who are to be ordained deacons and priests, and the prostration is made as described in number 681. After the prostration, the bishop, in a second monition, explains to the new subdeacons the functions of their order; then he causes them to touch the empty chalice with the paten, the cruets filled with water and wine; he clothes them with the amice, the maniple, and the tunic; and finally he causes them to touch the book of the Epistles, granting them the right to chant the Epistle at the Holy Sacrifice of the Mass.

683. *How is the ordination of deacons performed?*

Three things are to be noted in the ordination of deacons: (1) They are presented to the bishop by the archdeacon with a certain solemnity, because they are about to receive the imposition of hands. (2) The moment at which the bishop lays hands upon them is preceded by an admonition to the future deacons and by a Preface, which the pontiff completes after the imposition. (3) He lays one hand only upon the head of each, saying to each one: "Receive the Holy Ghost; may He be thy strength to withstand the devil and his temptations." — The bishop then vests the deacons with the stole and the dalmatic, and gives them the power to chant the Gospel, causing them to touch the book which contains it, or the missal.

684. *How is the ordination of priests performed?*

The priests, like the deacons, are solemnly presented to the bishop by the archdeacon. There are likewise two monitions: one addressed to the clergy and the people, the other to the ordinands. When the pontiff has concluded these admonitions, he lays both hands upon the head of each ordinand, and all the priests present do the same after him; then those same priests extend their right hand over the ordinands, as does the bishop, who at the same time recites a prayer in which he beseeches Almighty God to multiply His gifts upon those whom He has called to His priesthood.

After this, he chants a Preface which reiterates the same petitions, and then proceeds to the vesting of the new priests, which takes place before the consecration of the hands. For this, the pontiff crosses the stole over their breast and places the chasuble upon them, which remains folded in its back upper part until the end of the Mass. Then the *Veni Creator* is sung, during which the bishop consecrates the hands of each ordinand. He anoints the inside of the hands in the form of a cross with the oil of catechumens, then causes them to touch a chalice containing wine and a paten with a host, thereby giving to each priest the power to celebrate the Holy Sacrifice of the Mass. When all the ordinands have wiped off the oil from their hands and washed them, the bishop begins the prayers of the Offertory, which all the newly ordained priests recite aloud with him, as also the remainder of the Mass. Finally, after Holy Communion, the last ceremony of the ordination of priests is performed, which may be called the Mission. The new priests, standing before the pontiff, recite the Apostles' Creed, that profession of faith which they are henceforth to teach to the people. Then each one comes to kneel before the bishop, who gives him the power to forgive sins,[1] unfolds his chasuble, receives his promise

---

[1] It should be noted that the ceremonies which grant "the power to celebrated the Holy Sacrifice of the Mass" and "the power to forgive sins" are marking, by explicit ceremonies, powers already conferred on the newly ordained priests by the laying on of hands and the praying of the Preface. The same should be noted with regards to the ceremonies of the diaconate which make explicit the power conferred by the laying on of hands and the preface.

of obedience, and gives him the kiss of peace. Once the ordination is complete, it is customary to accompany the bishop back to his residence, or at least to the sacristy; this procession takes place to the chanting of the *Te Deum*, which the bishop intones at the foot of the altar.

§ IV.
OF THE CONSECRATION OF A BISHOP

685. *What are the most noteworthy elements in the consecration of a bishop, up to the Mass?*

One must note: (1) The solemn PRESENTATION of the bishop-elect. The two assisting bishops (who are required), vested in copes and wearing the simple miter, lead the elect, who is in a white cope with the biretta, and present him to the consecrator. The latter causes the apostolic letters authorizing the consecration to be read. (2) After this reading, the elect makes a particular oath of fidelity to Holy Church. (3) He undergoes what the Roman Pontifical calls the EXAMINATION. The consecrator questions the elect concerning the Faith; to each question, the elect rises, uncovers his head, and replies either *Credo*, "I believe it," or, when the question implies the will to practice a virtue, he replies *Volo*, "I will." (4) The examination ended, the elect prostrates himself with face to the ground at the left of the consecrator, and the Litany of the Saints is begun (see no. 681). — (5) When the prostration is complete, the consecrator begins a long Preface, which he interrupts midway to intone the *Veni Creator*. While it is being sung, he anoints the head of the elect in the form of a cross with the sacred chrism, and then spreads the anointing over the entire tonsure. The consecrator continues the Preface; when it is finished, he anoints the hands of the elect with the sacred chrism, after which the hands of the newly consecrated bishop are bound with a long linen cloth. Before the elect purifies his hands, the consecrator causes him to touch the crozier, places the ring upon his finger, has him touch the Book of the Gospels, and gives him the kiss of peace, as do also the two assistant bishops.

686. *What are the particular features of the Mass during the consecration of a bishop?*

When the consecration is complete, the newly consecrated bishop withdraws to the chapel that has been prepared for him; there his head and hands are purified, and he resumes the celebration of the Mass at the Offertory.[2] It is at this point that the offering takes place. The consecrated bishop, followed by acolytes, comes to kneel before the consecrator and presents him with two lit wax tapers, two small loaves, and two little barrels of wine one gilded, the other silvered; the same distinction applies to the loaves. After the offering, the newly consecrated bishop takes his place at the Epistle side, before his own missal which has been placed there for him, and continues the Mass with his consecrator. Two hosts and a double quantity of wine are placed

---

[2] In fact, after the Examination, the bishop-elect vests and begins to celebrate Mass in a side chapel in parallel with the consecrating bishop who is celebrating Mass at a separate altar.

in the chalice for the Communion of the two bishops. The newly consecrated bishop receives Holy Communion standing, from the hand of his consecrator, and under both species.[3] The Mass then proceeds as usual, and the consecrating bishop alone gives the final blessing to the people.

687. *How is the* enthronement *of the new bishop performed?*

Before the Last Gospel, the consecrator, seated in his chair and assisted by the assistant bishops, places the miter upon the head of the newly consecrated bishop, then the gloves and the ring. When this is done, the consecrator takes the bishop by the right hand, the first assistant bishop takes him by the left, and he is enthroned by being seated in the chair which the consecrator has just vacated, or even on the pontifical throne, if he has been consecrated in his own cathedral. Then the consecrator, bareheaded at the Gospel corner, intones the *Te Deum*. Once the hymn has begun, the newly consecrated bishop, placed between the two assistant bishops, all wearing miters, makes a circuit through the church, blessing the people. When he returns, and the hymn is ended, he gives a solemn blessing to the faithful. This august function concludes with the ceremony of the Farewell. The consecrator and the assistant bishops, all standing at the Gospel side with their miters, remain in place while the newly consecrated bishop, mitered and bearing

---

[3] By contrast, newly ordained priests receive, from the ordaining bishop, only the Host while kneeling—at the time of the priest's communion, not during the communion of the faithful.

the crozier, goes to the Epistle side. There he makes three genuflections toward the consecrator, advancing a few steps with each genuflection and singing each time with greater intensity: *Ad multos annos*, "Many years." After the third genuflection, the consecrator raises him, gives him the kiss of peace, as do the assistant bishops; the Last Gospel is then recited, and all depart in peace.

<h3 style="text-align:center">§ V.</h3>

OF THE CONSECRATION OF CHURCHES

688. *What are the principal ceremonies of the blessing of the first stone of a church?*

On the eve of the day on which this blessing is to take place, a cross is planted at the spot where the altar of the new church shall stand. — One must then note the blessing of the water,[4] the solemn blessing of the stone, which ought to be square in shape; the recitation of the Litanies, and the laying of the first stone by the bishop in the foundation, which he has thrice sprinkled while the antiphons and psalms, so wisely appointed by the Roman Church for this rite, are being chanted. The ceremony concludes with the chanting of the *Veni Creator* and the bishop's blessing.

689. *What are the most noteworthy ceremonies in the consecration of a church?*

This consecration begins with the recitation of the Penitential Psalms.[5] The faithful should then

---

[4] Called "Gregorian Water," which is specially blessed water mixed with blessed salt, blessed ashes, and wine.

[5] Psalms 6, 31, 37, 50, 101, 129, and 142.

take note of the following: (1) The triple aspersions of holy water made by the bishop, both outside the church and within, upon the walls, the cemetery or foundation ground, and the interior pavement. (2) The church door, kept shut, is opened at the sign of the cross made by the bishop with his crozier and at the threefold acclamation of the people: "Open! Open! Open!" — (3) The Greek and Latin alphabets traced upon ashes strewn in the form of a cross upon the floor of the church, to signify the union of the Latin and Greek Churches. (4) The five crosses frequently traced upon the altar to be consecrated, in memory of the Five Wounds of Our Lord; the relics of the saints placed within the altar; and the almost continual incensation of the altar, which represents Jesus Christ. (5) The procession of relics outside the church, and the entrance of the people behind the bishop once he has performed the anointing of the door with sacred chrism. (6) The consecration of the twelve pillars in honor of the twelve Apostles, the pillars of the Church. (7) Lastly, the Holy Sacrifice of the Mass offered upon the newly consecrated altar, to remind us that the Christian life cannot endure, nor attain perfection, without the immolation of the august Victim of our altars.

690. *What are the most noteworthy ceremonies in the blessing of a cemetery?*

Four crosses are placed at the extremities of the cemetery,[6] and a larger one in the center. At

---

[6] The four corner crosses are no longer required in the simplified ceremony of 1961.

the time of the blessing, three candles burn before each of these five crosses. The Litany of the Saints are recited, along with the Penitential Psalms and others with their proper antiphons. Between these psalms, the bishop chants solemn prayers; then he blesses and incenses, one by one, the five crosses of the cemetery and the ground itself, and concludes by imparting his blessing to the people. Afterwards, having returned to the church, he either celebrates the Holy Sacrifice of the Mass himself, or has it celebrated by a priest.

691. *What is to be said concerning the blessing of bells?*

This was spoken of under number 48. — It suffices to note that this blessing is reserved to bishops. However, a priest may perform it with the express authorization of the Ordinary.

Appendix II

✠

ECCLESIASTICAL CHANT[†]

OF ECCLESIASTICAL CHANT

692. *What is chant?*

It is a succession of diverse sounds whose harmony pleases and serves to express or awaken the movements of the soul.

693. *Why is chant employed in the offices of the Church?*

In order to bring into relief the truths conveyed by the liturgical words, and to stir in souls the sentiments that correspond thereto: prayer, joy, holy sorrow, according to the circumstances.

694. *Does any sort of chant fulfill this end?*

That which stifles the words beneath a crash of sound, that which arouses the passions rather than the affections of the soul, cannot rightly be called religious chant.

695. *Does the Church possess a chant proper to Herself?*

---

† This text was read at the Religious Music Congress held in Rodez, from July 22 to 25, 1895 (original editor's note by Abbé Vigourel). In the original French, the numbering of points started over here, but in this English edition, the numbering of questions has been continued in sequence for the reader's convenience.

The Church presents us in Her liturgical books with melodies superimposed upon the liturgical texts. Their ensemble constitutes Gregorian chant.

696. *Why is it called Gregorian chant?*

Because Saint Gregory I the Great, pope from 590 to 604, gave to the chants of the pontifical basilica a form that has remained definitive.

697. *How was this chant gradually adopted throughout nearly the whole Latin Church?*

Through the natural desire to imitate the Mother Church, and also on account of its intrinsic worth.

698. *To what is this worth to be attributed?*

The Church of Rome was, as it were, the natural confluence of Jewish, Greek, and Roman art. Saint Gregory, in addition to a particular assistance of the Holy Ghost, had received in Rome the benefit of the most distinguished education. He was admirably prepared to gather up the purest conceptions which ancient musical art had inspired in the Christians of the early centuries.

699. *Who introduced this form of chant into France?*

It was Pepin and Charlemagne. They brought masters from Rome. Charlemagne employed, in particular, the diffusion of this sacred music to soften little by little the barbarous customs of the newly converted. The liturgy, in his mind, was the most efficacious means of civilization.

700. *Was Gregorian chant preserved in France?*

Not only was it preserved, but it was enriched. In recent times it has been possible to reconstitute the artistic treasures held in our libraries from a musical point of view. The Gregorian work remained intact until the fifteenth century. Moreover, a rich flowering of proses, hymns, antiphons, and responsories was added thereto, filling our ancient medieval cathedrals with musical garlands as splendid as their stone lacework and their sparkling windows.

701. *Does our present plainchant give us a true idea of the Church's chant?*

If it is rendered with taste, with piety, and by well-trained voices, if it is not drowned beneath an accompaniment that destroys its character, it still retains admirable beauties. It may be likened to our noble Gothic churches, disfigured no doubt by the vandalism of revolutions, but great and proud still, in the midst of the too often paltry productions of modern art.

702. *How could the Church have allowed the rich treasure she had formed to be lost for a time?*

The Church can lose nothing of her doctrinal treasures. But in the means she employs to lead souls to God, she can adapt to the conditions of the times.[1]

703. *How were these conditions altered?*

The development of polyphonic music, or that with several simultaneous voices, gradually

---

[1] Implied: and thus, can adapt well or poorly, and if the latter, reform is needed.

caused the free rhythm of Gregorian chant to be lost. It thus became a body without a soul.

704. *Where is this loss of rhythm most noticeable?*

In certain pieces: the Graduals and the Alleluias, for example, where the expression of sentiment had become predominant.

705. *Can you explain this point to us?*

In these passages, a single word gives rise to the soul's outpourings, pious movements of prayer, of joy, of confidence, of humility, of love. The melody then casts off the restraints of articulation: it retains only the subtlest element of the word, the vowel, with its manifold timbres. Hence those sometimes very lengthy series, wherein the breath of the soul must pour itself forth, as an artist draws forth its tremor upon the strings of his violin, or in the vibrations now gentle, now powerful of the organ. These vocalizations thus lost their rhythm.

706. *What was the result of this change in execution?*

When heavily chanted, with the groups disjoined into a kind of solemn spelling, these long sequences of disconnected notes inspired only boredom and distaste.

707. *What did the Church do then?*

Since these melodies no longer fulfilled their purpose, the Church was compelled to suppress them and seek elsewhere a means of lifting souls to God. Hence arose those editions of chant in which numerous pieces, now abridged, have lost what was most artistic in them. And even then, such abbreviations were most often made at random, by the snip of scissors in the hands of musicians who lacked the Gregorian sense, by then generally lost. Hoping to infuse new life into the Offices, men turned to polyphonic music.

708. *What disadvantage resulted from this?*

A disadvantage against which ecclesiastical authority has never ceased to protest: the abuses of polyphonic music. Too often, there remained no distinction between so-called Church music and secular music save the personal taste of the composer or the listener; and thus, there was no safeguard against the incursion of the theater into the Church. This incursion was all the more to be feared since modern music, by its incomparable resources of harmony and instrumentation, acts powerfully upon the senses, excels in expressing and exciting the passions, and therefore ever lends itself to the confusion between true religious sentiment and a vague sentimentality, more apt to make dilettantes than Christians.

709. *What are the advantages of Gregorian chant when well executed?*

I. The assurance that it is certainly religious.

II. The certainty that it will not harm the text with which, by the authority of the Church, it is intimately united.

III. The ease of execution, even in the humblest parishes, since the only instrument required is the human voice.

IV. Finally, it becomes popular wherever it is well chanted, something which cannot be said of learned music.

710. *May one hope for the revival of true Gregorian chant?*

Since it is one of the treasures of the Roman Church, one may well hope that she shall know how to make use of it when an intelligent execution shall have restored to it the virtue it possessed in the ages of faith.[2] Today, our age has once more understood and admired the architecture, the literature, and all the other arts of the Middle Ages; the Sovereign Pontiff has restored her philosophy to honor, why should musical art alone remain unrecognized? It has now been rediscovered; it only remains to make it known.

711. *What course should be followed while awaiting a formal approval?*

Nothing prevents, first of all, the application of a sound method to the chant-books currently in use. One may also perform a selection of pieces drawn from the ancient liturgical books, just as one does with the productions of modern music.

712. *What is the generating principle of the rules of execution by which Gregorian chant may be rendered in all its worth?*

---

[2] On November 22, 1903, soon after Abbé Vigourel's Appendix II was delivered and published, Pius X issued the motu proprio *Tra le sollecitudini*. His decision to reinstate the ancient traditional Gregorian chant in the entire Church was influenced by the successful restoration of the purest form of plainchant by Solesmes Abbey under such well-known musicians as Dom Paul Jausions (1834–1870), Dom Joseph Pothier (1835–1923), and Dom Andrew Mocquereau (1849–1930), the real founder of the choir of Solesmes. On the teaching of Pius X, see Patrick J. Brill, *The Great Sacred Music Reform of Pope St. Pius X: The Genesis, Interpretation, and Implementation of the Motu Proprio* Tra le Sollecitudini (Os Justi Press, 2025).

Since the texts of liturgical chant are generally in Latin prose, the rules of execution, first applied at Solesmes, are derived from the rules for reading Latin.

713. *What are the advantages of this method?*

It is the most logical and the most simple; very easy for less ornate pieces, and the only method truly effective in revealing the beauties of the more elaborate melodies preserved in the manuscripts.

714. *Could you indicate the most important of these rules?*

One distinguishes between general rules and particular rules. The following are those which several major seminaries have adopted:

I. General Rules

Ecclesiastical chants consist in a body of Latin texts melodically expressed in order to *praise God, to enlighten, and to move souls.* From the nature and the purpose of these chants arises the obligation to *pronounce the Latin well,* to *sing correctly,* and to chant in a *spirit of reverence.*

1. *To pronounce the Latin well, one must:*
    a) Give to the vowels their proper *timbre;*
    b) *Articulate* the consonants distinctly;
    c) Preserve the unity of each word by a precise and well-marked *accentuation;*
    d) *Phrase* grammatically, that is, to group together the words forming a single member of a sentence, and to separate the various members of

a sentence from one another, in such a way as to bring out the meaning of the chanted text.

2. *To sing correctly, one must:*

a) Follow the *rules proper to each kind* of chant;

b) Conform to the *particular* customs of the place where the chant is being sung;

c) *Not sing from memory*, but follow exactly in the book both the text and the notation being executed;

d) Attend to the *ensemble*: watch for the signal of the intonation, listen to the others, and maintain the given impetus without delay or precipitation;

e) Govern one's voice well: moderate it; never force the breath, but rather restrain it; vary the intensity and movement of the voice according to the demands of the piece;

f) *Breathe appropriately*: take a quick breath at minor bars, a full breath at major bars and mediant pauses; employ deep or diaphragmatic breathing to store up greater reserves of breath;

g) *Soften the final notes* and prolong them slightly, so that the cessation of the voice may occur without abruptness.

3. *To sing religiously, one must:*

a) Enter into *recollection* before beginning, in order to awaken in the soul pious sentiments in harmony with the feast being celebrated and with the liturgical text about to be chanted;

b) Perform the chant as an act of *praise* and *prayer*;

c) Avoid all that might seem *abrupt, pretentious,* or tinged with a *sentimentality* of poor taste.

II. Particular Rules

1. *Simple Recitation and Psalmody*

Prayers recited in common and the various parts of the Divine Office must be rendered with unity and correctness. To that end:

* All should begin together;
* adopt the same pitch;
* listen to one another;
* follow the same rhythm;
* distinguish the words by means of proper accentuation;
* separate the members of the sentence;
* in the psalms, mark the mediant with a brief pause;
* recite each half-verse in a single breath.

2. *Solemn Recitation*

This occurs in the chanting of versicles, orations, the Epistle, the Gospel, and the lessons. One must:

* Observe the rules of reading: accentuation, grouping of words, and separation of sentence-members;
* give the voice greater amplitude and adopt a slower pace than in simple recitation;
* chant the versicles in one continuous phrase, without a break in the middle;
* soften the cadences at the ends of versicles and lessons;
* in Hebrew words, place the cadence on the penultimate syllable.

3. *The Chanting of the Psalms*

The beauty of the psalms depends first upon

unity of execution, then upon the proper rendering of mediants and cadences.

a) To ensure *unity*:

* all must begin together;
* chant each half-verse in a single breath;
* clearly mark the accented syllables;
* suspend the voice and take a deep breath at the mediant;
* begin each verse as soon as the other choir has finished the preceding verse, yet without haste.

b) To ensure the *proper rendering of mediants and cadences*:

* learn the particular characteristics of each mode of plainchant;
* note, in one's chant book, the chief faults to be avoided in the psalms most frequently used;
* indicate the syllables upon which the *elevation* must occur before the accented syllable:

    1. in the mediant of the 3rd and 7th modes, of the 1st Gregorian mode, and of the solemn 5th mode;

    2. in the cadences of the 7th and 5th modes;

* bear in mind that the aforesaid elevation is made on the second syllable before the final accented syllable, unless that syllable ends the word or is a short penult.

4. Syllabic Chants

This term refers to those pieces in which each syllable generally corresponds to a single note: such as hymns, proses, the Preface, the *Pater noster*, etc. In order to execute them well:

* Follow the rules of reading: maintain a fairly brisk pace, observe correct accentuation;

❋ group the words according to their meaning: do not breathe between two syllables of the same word, nor even between two words that the sense binds together;

❋ assign to the notes a duration roughly equal in time;

❋ vary their intensity according to the rules of accentuation.

5. *Ornamented and Neumatic Chants*
These occur in antiphons, Introits, etc., where a single vowel is often extended through a series of notes. This series is called a *group, formula,* or *neume.*

a) To *preserve the unity of the vowel*:

❋ perform the entire formula in a single emission of the voice;

❋ emphasize the first note more strongly, and glide through the others, giving to each approximately the same duration.

b) To *preserve the unity of the word*:

❋ join closely to the following syllable of the same word the final note of the preceding syllable;

❋ do not prolong that note;

❋ never breathe before pronouncing the next syllable of a word already begun (*the rule of unity*).

6. *Series of Groups and Melismas*
In the *Kyrie,* Graduals, Alleluias, etc., a single vowel may be extended over a sometimes very long succession of neumes. In order to bring out the rhythm, which is the source of their beauty, one must:

❋ distinguish the groups by slightly emphasizing the first note of each formula;

❊ prolong the final note of each group, though this prolongation should be slight between connected groups, and more pronounced between isolated groups;

❊ slow the final group to prepare for the repose;

❊ give to all the notes approximately equal duration.

In Benedictine books, the formulas are grouped according to the natural proportions of the rhythm. In books where the notes are evenly spaced, the groups must be anticipated and clearly marked.

III. Rules for Accentuation

1. *Nature of the accent*

Words derive their unity from the accent, which is the center and soul of the word. — In *French*, the final syllable bears the accent, unless it is mute. — In *Latin*, the final syllable is always softened; the same is true of the penultimate, if it is prosodically short. But the accent never retreats beyond the antepenultimate syllable. The accented syllable is at once a support and a rise: it ought not to be prolonged.

2. *Placement of the accent*

a) *Monosyllables* are accented, except for prepositions, conjunctions, and certain relative pronouns.

b) In *disyllabic* words, the accent always falls on the first syllable. However, the name *Jesús* and indeclinable Hebrew words such as *Jacób*, *Joséph*, *Amén*, etc., are accented on the final syllable.[3]

---

[3] In 1912, the Sacred Congregation of Rites allowed the accent of monosyllabic words to be ignored and Hebrew words to be

c) In words of *more than two syllables*, the accent is placed on the penultimate syllable when it is long, and on the antepenultimate when the penultimate is short.

d) The particles *que, ne, ve*, when occurring at the end of words, draw the accent onto the syllable immediately preceding them. Example: *armáque, pluítne*.

3. *Quantity of the penultimate syllable*

a) A diphthong is always long and consequently accented. Example: *æ* in *Judæa*.

b) A vowel followed by another vowel is almost always short. Example: *spiritui, gloria*. — There are exceptions in certain words derived from Hebrew or Greek. Example: *María, platéa, bravíum, prophetía, litanía…*

c) A vowel followed by a double consonant (*x, z*), or by two consonants of which the second is not *l* or *r*, is always long. Example: *baptízo, crucifíxus, dedístis*.

d) The infinitives of verbs have the penultimate syllable long in all conjugations except the third. Thus: *amáre, monére, audíre*, but: *légere*.

e) The imperfect tense of active verbs always has the penultimate long: *amábam, monébant, legébant*.

f) Likewise, the third person plural of all perfect indicatives in the active voice: *amavérunt, legérunt*.

---

pronounced accented on the penultimate syllable in liturgical recitation.

If you enjoyed this work, you might enjoy some of Os Justi Press's other books on liturgical history and tradition

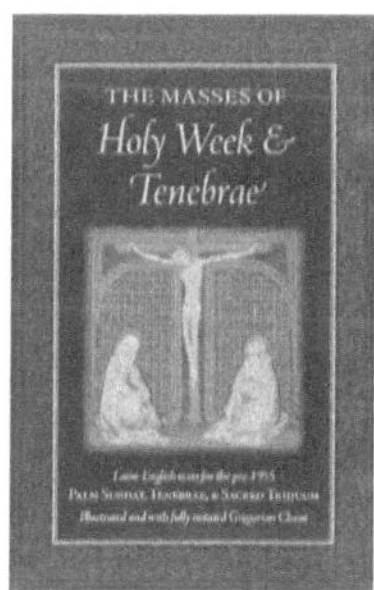

The Masses of Holy Week & Tenebrae

Liturgical Institutions

Lumen Christi

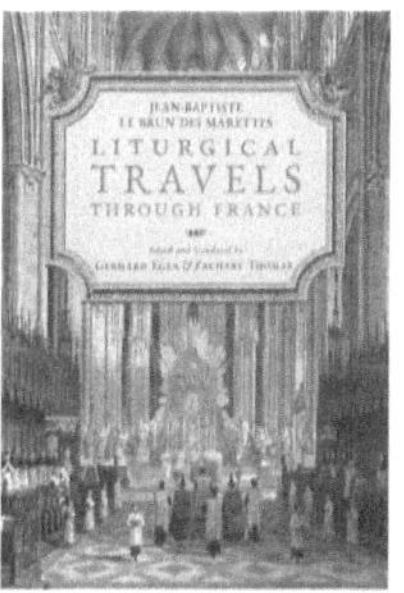

Liturgical Travels

The Mass in Transition

Sacred Signs

*Christian Life
and Worship*

*The Holy Sacrifice
of the Mass*

The Life of Worship

The Fulness of Sacrifice

The Breviary Explained

Sacred and Great

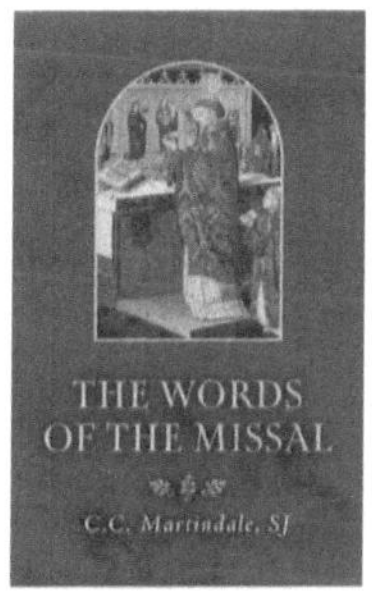

The Words of the Missal

Latin in Church

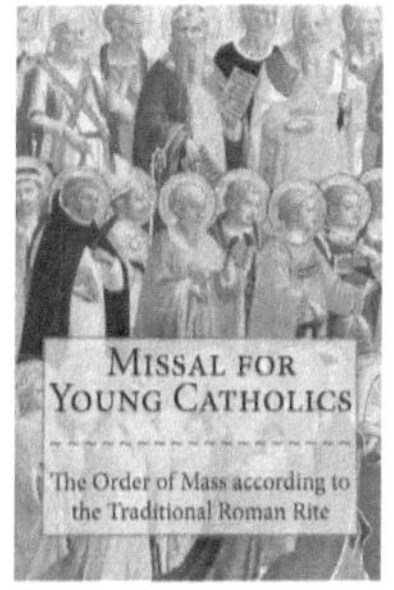

*Missal for
Young Catholics*

Thomistic Mystagogy

*The Message of the
Mass Melodies*

*Illusions
of Reform*

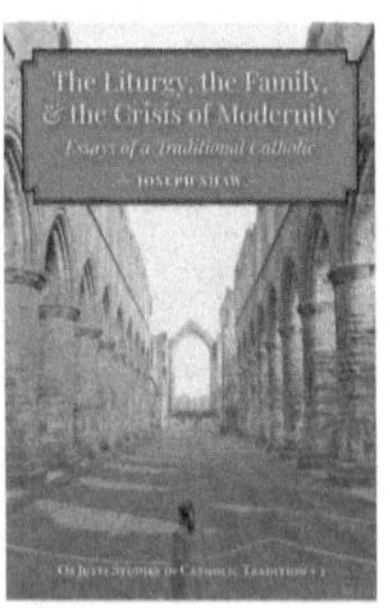

*The Liturgy, the
Family, and the
Crisis of Modernity*

*The Great Sacred
Music Reform of
Pope St. Pius X*